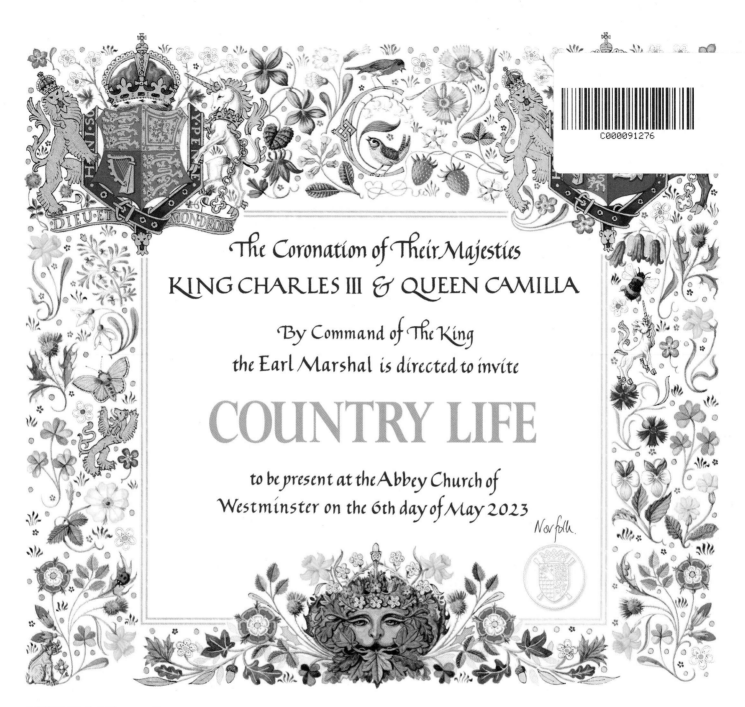

The Coronation of Their Majesties

KING CHARLES III & QUEEN CAMILLA

By Command of The King
the Earl Marshal is directed to invite

COUNTRY LIFE

to be present at the Abbey Church of
Westminster on the 6th day of May 2023

Norfolk.

Contents

Front cover:
The King in the Throne Room (2023 Hugo Burnand Ltd).
Top: **The Coronation Invitation (Raj Valley/Alamy).**
Back cover: **The King and Queen (2023 Hugo Burnand Ltd)**

Future Publishing Ltd, 121–141 Westbourne Terrace, Paddington, London W2 6JR

0330 390 6591; www.countrylife.co.uk

Crowned under the gaze of the world

After the longest wait in history, The King has shown that he is more than ready to lead, says **Clive Aslet**

FORGET for a moment the golden carriages, the horses, plumes, robes, trumpets, Bryn Terfel and the Garter King at Arms. All the grand ceremonial of the coronation made a magnificent spectacle; yet, for now, let us strip it away and remember that, at the centre of it all, is the single human being who has been crowned King. We have in him not only an ermine-robed figurehead, holding orb and sceptre, but an extraordinary individual. All kings are, of course, extraordinary through their exalted office. This one, however, is remarkable for the long apprenticeship that he has had to the role.

As the oldest British monarch to ascend the throne, he has necessarily spent the most time of any in preparing for it. Inheriting the throne at 25, Her late Majesty, Queen Elizabeth II, radiated the freshness of youth and learnt as she went along. Charles III is 74. As well as his mother's sense of duty, he brings to the role a lifetime's experience, shaped by continuous travel, constant interaction with the cleverest and most talented people around the globe and his own reading and reflection. His knowledge of the world may be particular, but it is also unique.

No individual is perfect. In the annals of monarchy, there have been more monsters than saints. After the death of Diana, Princess of Wales, some pundits said that the Prince of Wales should have forfeited his right to the succession in favour of his eldest son; it was maintained that Camilla would never become Queen. However, the disasters of the past have been overcome and now serve to put His Majesty in a more human light. Families are not perfect. Marriages do not always run according to plan. Many people have

embarrassing brothers or disobliging sons; they may get cross with leaky fountain pens. Royalty—as Prince Harry understands—is in the celebrity business. It must live continually in the media spotlight, which harshly magnifies every weakness and misrepresents many actions. Fortunately for traditionalists, Charles III overcame his sour-minded critics, rose above their carping and, after decades in waiting, had the crown placed upon his head. The fact that it was predicted (by some) never to happen made the occasion doubly triumphant.

Television commentary focused largely on the splendour of the event. Readers who want to understand more about the history and meaning of the ritual and regalia need Sir Roy Strong's *Coronation*, first published in 2005 and newly reissued with an epilogue. Everything is explained, from the symbolic meaning of function to the history of the Stone of Scone, presented to the shrine of Edward the Confessor in Westminster Abbey by Edward I. This legend-encrusted block of red sandstone, also known as the Stone of Destiny, was placed inside the Coronation Chair made specially to contain it—a wooden pattern for what was intended to have been a bronze version, before the costly process of casting was abandoned due to the expense of the wars in France. (When the stone was returned to Scotland by John Major in 1996 ahead of devolution, 'a unique medieval artefact was vandalised,' wrote Sir Roy.) In Charles III's coronation, the ancient roots of kingship were further emphasised by the appearance of the sixth-century Gospels of St Augustine, the oldest surviving Latin Gospels in the world, which were brought from Corpus Christi College, Cambridge, at the special request of His Majesty.

Much has been said about the new aspects of this coronation—the Gospel singing, Greek chanting and general air of inclusiveness (tiaras were not worn). In truth, every coronation is different from its predecessors. The liturgy had to be revived by the Oxford Movement in the 19th century. Not all coronations have been successes. When William the Conqueror was crowned, the shout of acclamation by the crowd outside Westminster Abbey was taken to be the beginning of a revolt and the army set fire to London. The singing of Handel's anthems for George II's coronation was chaotic, with, at one point, two choirs attempting different anthems at the same time. Queen Victoria's ring was forced onto the wrong finger by the Archbishop.

No such muddle attended proceedings on May 6. It was glorious, not only in its colour and royal theatre, but in the discipline that underpinned the whole complex operation. Even the erection of the screen that guarded the Anointment from the eyes of the world was performed with military drill. No detail had been overlooked. Politics may be a shambles and covid lockdowns have undermined the willingness of some people to turn up to a place of work. Happily, however, there remains one area of national life that runs on time, due to the immense efforts of the participants. Discipline is what the nation expects—and gets—from the monarch, his heir apparent and those who serve them. This was the subliminal message that the coronation broadcast to the world.

> **‘The King's knowledge of the world may be particular, but it is also unique’**

Editor	Picture Editor	Chief Sub-Editor	Head of Design	Senior Designer
Paula Lester	Lucy Ford	Octavia Pollock	Dean Usher	Ben Harris
Deputy Editor	**Deputy Picture Editor**	**Associate Editor**	**Deputy Art Editor**	**Editorial Assistant**
James Fisher	Emily Anderson	Agnes Stamp	Heather Clark	Amie Elizabeth White

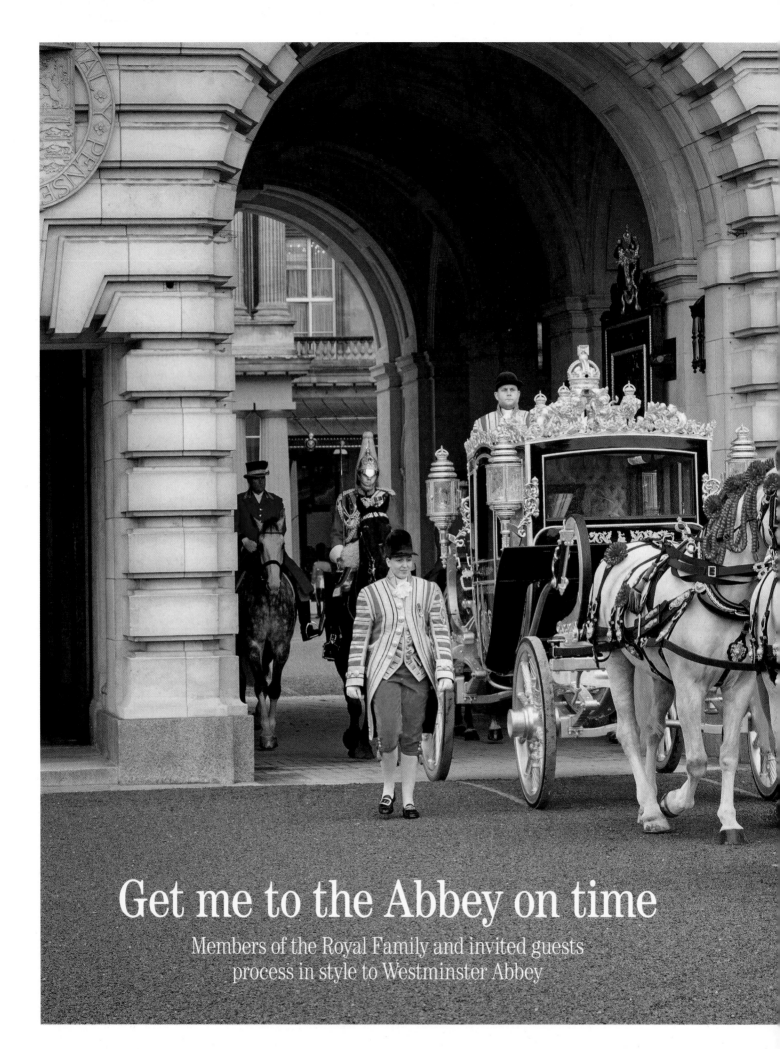

Get me to the Abbey on time

Members of the Royal Family and invited guests
process in style to Westminster Abbey

The Diamond Jubilee State Coach, drawn by six Windsor Greys, leaves Buckingham Palace. The carriage, built in 2012 in Australia to mark 60 years of the late Queen's reign, is air conditioned, built on an aluminium frame and is adorned with a crown carved from oak from the oldest warship in the world still in commission, HMS *Victory*

A sea of footguards: the Household Division is responsible for delivering state ceremonial and public duties, primarily in London and Windsor. Its headquarters is at Horse Guards on Whitehall

The Prince of Wales arrives in the ceremonial dress uniform of the Welsh Guards, to represent his role as Colonel of the Regiment. Beneath her royal-blue ceremonial robes, The Princess of Wales wore an ivory silk caped gown designed by Sarah Burton, creative director of Alexander McQueen

The King's niece, Zara Tindall

Princess Charlotte holds her younger brother Prince Louis's hand in the Abbey

The King's sister, Anne, The Princess Royal

Princess Beatrice

Prince Harry, the Duke of Sussex

The Duchess of Edinburgh and Lady Louise

Prince George served as a Page of Honour

The Lady Helen Taylor

Australian musician Nick Cave

Felipe VI of Spain and Queen Letizia

Singer and songwriter Lionel Richie

Rishi Sunak and Akshata Murthy

Actress Emma Thompson

Finnegan Biden and First Lady Jill Biden

Brigitte and Emmanuel Macron

Justin and Sophie Grégoire Trudeau

Actress and broadcaster Joanna Lumley ♛

Long live our noble King!

Could anyone who watched King Charles being crowned fail to have been moved by the sheer spectacle and the cultural significance of a man finally fulfilling his destiny, asks **Matthew Dennison**

TO the golden chain of monarchy in these islands has been added another link. A king is crowned and, in his person, past, present and future combine. In Westminster Abbey, on a day of intermittent, soft grey rain, ancient ritual, his own prayers and the hopes of a watching nation confirmed King Charles III, in the words of the Archbishop of Canterbury, as 'set apart'. And in homes and village halls, community centres and public parks, in the United Kingdom and the Commonwealth and to the furthest ends of the inhabited earth, were those who joined with the Abbey congregation in the age-old prayer: *God Save The King.*

Could any heart have witnessed so extraordinary a spectacle unmoved, any voice remain quite steady, any eye dry? Bare headed, the newly anointed King knelt before the altar. He was a man like any other, but one called to a destiny beyond the comprehension of the many watching millions. He had prayed aloud that, in God's service, he might find knowledge of God's truth in a life now formally bound to others' wellbeing—and none could doubt his sincerity. →

The Armills, 'bracelets of sincerity and wisdom', borne by Lord Kamall

Penny Mordaunt, the Lord President of the Council, wields the Jewelled Sword of Offering, having relinquished the Sword of State

Dame Elizabeth Anionwu, a former nurse, with the Sovereign's Orb

The King presents the Sword of Offering to the Dean of Westminster, Dr David Hoyle, at the altar

A coronation is a marker on history's long road, the trumpet blast that proclaims a new epoch and, in 2023, a third Carolean age. Its time-honoured rites serve, too, to remind us of those who have gone before: the shimmering continuum of kings and queens of these islands, all of whom, since the Norman Conquest, have been crowned in the same magnificent cathedral church. At the centre of the gorgeous whirligig on Saturday was our King of nine months, a son, grandson and great-grandson of the House of Windsor. From Saturday's ceremony, he emerged, said the Archbishop, 'consecrated for the service of his people'. He was also, undoubtedly, transformed by an experience that was both intensely personal and unrelentingly public.

By Wednesday morning of the preceding week, a mushroom crop of tiny tents punctuated the long stretch of the Mall, where the tall flags of the Commonwealth hung from crown-topped posts. So swollen were the numbers of spectators gathered along the route by Saturday that police turned late-comers away. Disappointing weather—an echo of the late Queen's coronation on an unseasonably cold June day 70 years before— did not dispirit crowds as varied in background and origin as the congregation inside the Abbey. Their cheers accompanied the King and Queen on all three of their journeys—from Clarence House to Buckingham Palace, where they changed into their coronation robes; from the Palace to Westminster Abbey, riding in the Diamond Jubilee State Coach; and from the Abbey back to the Palace, in the famous Gold State Coach designed by William Chambers for the coronation of George III.

' He was transformed by an experience that was both intensely personal and unrelentingly public '

Of course, gainsayers had derided this day of days. Some, echoing Labour Party co-founder Keir Hardie at the time of George V's coronation in 1911, had protested at 'an orgy for the display of wealth and senseless spending'. Others forecast indifference, protests, demonstrations—but it was affection and, in so many cases, love, that gripped the capital's streets; and love, pride and a sense of wonder experienced by many among the 300 million who, in four corners of the globe, tuned in to witness these ancient rites. In Britain, wrote Prince Christopher of Greece in 1938, 'you find this personal love of the Sovereign and his family, a sentiment that passes even fidelity; a perfect understanding. Monarchy… is ingrained in the hearts of the people'. Clear to many was the survival of this personal love felt by men, women and children for Britain's newest sovereign.

Inside the Abbey for The King and Queen's arrival at 11am, heralded by peals of bells, were more than 2,200 people, from more than 200 countries. Among them were royal guests from three continents, including, in a break from tradition, fellow crowned heads. As a reflection of distinctly 21st-century preoccupations, media attention focused on a small contingent of famous faces, but this was far from a celebrity →

Facing page: **The two Sceptres, with Cross and Dove, have spiritual significance.** *Above:* **A tender moment between father and son**

harlequinade. The King was crowned in a Christian ceremony that celebrated God's glory and His timeless example of loving service; The King and Queen received communion and, presenting His Majesty with a specially bound Bible, commissioned by Lambeth Palace, the Moderator of the General Assembly of the Church of Scotland told The King: 'Here is Wisdom… these are the lively oracles of God.' Sacred music filled the Abbey's soaring spaces, its selection by His Majesty—including the new works he had commissioned himself—testament to his own deeply held faith. Among the coronation's many innovations was the King's prayer, spoken aloud, that he be 'a blessing to all [God's] children, of every faith and belief'.

For this, as never before in British history, was the coronation of a king whose subjects are of many faiths and none. Sturdy in its Protestant avowals, the service was the most ecumenical ever witnessed. For the first time since the Reformation, prominent Roman Catholic clergy were present; in the new Cross of Wales, a gift from the Church in Wales and carried in The King's Procession, were fragments of the True Cross, given to His Majesty by the Pope. Sacred music included Elizabethan recusant William Byrd's setting of words from the Edwardian Protestant Book of Common Prayer, *Prevent us, O Lord.*

> **Sturdy in its Protestant avowals, the service was the most ecumenical ever witnessed**

The merging of Anglican and Catholic in the anthem's genesis typified the spiritual generosity of a service that affirmed the monarch's role as Supreme Governor of the Church of England, yet acknowledged the diverse beliefs of His Majesty's subjects: in the processions and presentations were Hindu, Sikh and Jewish life peers and representatives of Judaism, Sikhism, Hinduism, Islam and Buddhism greeted their crowned King.

In his sermon, the Archbishop of Canterbury told listeners: 'What is given today is for the gain of all.' That The King intended to be crowned a king for all his subjects was consistently clear. The Kyrie Eleison was sung in Welsh; after the Archbishop's sermon, the choir sang a setting of *Veni, Creator Spiritus* in the four languages of the Union, all but the 17th-century English translation new commissions. As 70 years ago, guests from across the Commonwealth occupied many of the Abbey's seats and stalls. At the beginning of this great occasion, a procession of representatives of the 14 Commonwealth Realms, bright flags borne aloft, reminded those watching that Britons share their king with millions of people across the world. Some of those scattered multitudes may sever their ties with the Crown. In the meantime, their presence indicated the scale of this royal inheritance and Charles III's challenges.   →

Above: **The royal congregation.** *Facing page:* **The newly crowned King and Queen listen to Andrew Lloyd-Webber's setting of Psalm 98**

In 1953, playwright Noël Coward applauded 'the English state ballet at its best': a display of pageantry that encompassed the Royal Watermen in new scarlet uniforms, marching Gurkha pipers, Canadian mounties, troops from 'the Colonies'. Seven decades later, those roles and ranks were represented again and the cavalcade, albeit smaller, was every bit as impressive. The King is head of the Armed Forces; among the regalia presented to him were golden spurs, armills and a jewelled sword, symbols of the knightly power of medieval kings. Uniforms filled the streets, uniforms filled the Abbey. The power of earlier kings was absolute: our newest King's power lies in leading by example, in embodying the truism articulated by the Archbishop that 'service is love in action'.

> ‘ **Our King's power lies in leading by example, in embodying the truism that "service is love in action"** ’

An ancient patchwork, its roots in the ninth century, codified over succeeding centuries, the Coronation Service has survived in outline since King Edgar was crowned in Bath Abbey in May 973. Edgar inherited the throne as a young man; Charles III is the oldest person to take on his royal destiny, but the rituals of his crowning resembled Edgar's in each essential. Key elements shaped the service. At the Recognition, The King was presented to the congregation and bowed to north, south, east and west, 'undoubted king' of every point of the compass. In his Oath, he made promises about his kingship. The most sacred moment was the Anointing. Concealed from view behind embroidered screens, His Majesty sat in the Coronation Chair above an inlaid Cosmati stone pavement commissioned for the Abbey by Henry III 800 years ago. Its dulled jewel colours depict the world on the Day of Judgement, awaiting Christ's merciful justice, and the Archbishop touched The King's hands, head and breast with holy oil. It is a ritual as old as the Old Testament in which Zadok the Priest anoints Solomon and it was accompanied by Handel's magnificent anthem celebrating Zadok's wisdom, written for George II. The anointed King received the Coronation Regalia, a gifting known as the Investiture; he was crowned in the Coronation Chair. A crash of gun salutes, the ringing of the bells, a fanfare and, from across the Abbey, from those close and distant, a cry of 'God Save The King' accompanied the Archbishop placing on His Majesty's head the golden St Edward's Crown made for Charles II.

It was the making of history, the confirmation of a new monarch's embracing of a burden of service unimaginable in its weight: proof a new reign had begun. The Prince of Wales paid Homage to his father. In the congregation, across the UK and beyond, others made voluntary promises of faithfulness. It was a moment of transformation for subjects as well as sovereign. →

The King had been dressed in priestly garments. 'May the Lord clothe you with the robe of righteousness,' the Archbishop prayed, and the sacerdotal quality of His Majesty's clothes suggested vocation, his out-of-the-ordinary calling. The golden Supertunica was made for the coronation of his great-grandfather, George V, in 1911, and was worn by George VI and Elizabeth II. Its symbolism confirmed His Majesty's legitimacy, his place in the sequence of much-loved sovereigns who have shaped modern monarchy in this country, as he himself will do. For the moment of crowning, he wore the Royal Robe or Imperial Mantle, woven 200 years ago for the coronation of George IV. This garment of medieval splendour recalled the golden cloaks worn by the priests who, in the Liber Regalis, or Royal Book, of 1382, crowned Richard II and his Queen, Anne of Bohemia. Visual symbolism shaped much of The King's coronation. Repeatedly it asserted monarchy's long sway in these islands, and our new King's place in a line broken only once, briefly, in the middle of the 17th century.

' In the ancient Abbey precincts, vivid as tapestry emerged a glittering picture of 21st-century Britain '

For months, commentators had speculated on the likely form His Majesty's coronation would take. Much was made of a 'slimmed-down' ceremony, smaller in scale, shorter in duration, of fewer guests, accompanied in all ways by less fanfaronade than the coronation of 1953. Yet here were such riches, in a service marked by faith and thoughtfulness, powerful in its endorsement of loving service. Inclusion and diversity, buzzwords of the age, were embraced with joy and sincerity. In the ancient Abbey precincts, vivid as tapestry emerged a glittering picture of 21st-century Britain. As in a tapestry, different threads were woven into a harmonious whole and men and women distinct in race, ethnicity, faith and gender came together in a shared act of celebration and national rededication. Here was hope, aspiration and confidence. Here was the trumpet blast of the new Carolean age.

At His Majesty's side throughout was Her Majesty the Queen, crowned with the crown made for Queen Mary in 1911 and wearing a gown embroidered with flowers of the Commonwealth and those of her wedding bouquet, as well as her Jack Russell terriers, Bluebell and Beth. The King's reign encompasses many partnerships, but none more precious to him than the loving support of his wife, Camilla. Her own family were prominent in the service and its congregation, as were members of the Royal Family, yet the final picture of an historic day was of the royal couple, robed and crowned, alone on the balcony of Buckingham Palace. Their reign will not, like that of Elizabeth II, extend into a new century. But it will bless the present and, from across the United Kingdom and the Commonwealth, rise prayers for its prosperity and long continuance. ♔

Bearing the Orb and Sceptre with Cross, The King is flanked by the Bishops of Durham and Bath and Wells

Their crowning glory

When Charles III felt the weight of St Edward's Crown, he felt the weight of centuries. It is to this most familiar attribute of royalty, heavy with gold and glittering jewels, that we owe allegiance, explains **Matthew Dennison**

Queen Camilla wears Queen Mary's Crown, made for the wife of George V and re-set for 2023 with the Cullinan III, IV and V diamonds

THE hand that descends from heaven holds above the king's head a golden circlet. Jewels stud the sturdy band, alternating egg- and lozenge-shaped knuckle dusters. To the monarch's left and right, in this 9th-century illustration of the coronation of the Frankish ruler Charles the Bald from a manuscript in Paris's Bibliothèque Nationale, stand bishops. Their gaze does not dwell on the king himself. Instead, it is the crown that transfixes their attention. At this moment of royal transformation, the crown embodies Charles's pre-eminence. Above it is a cross, which, like the crown, is golden, gleaming.

Nothing expresses earthly kingship more powerfully than a crown. As an emblem of royalty and divinely ordained authority, it was assumed in evocation of Old Testament references by Byzantine Emperors from the 4th century. Charlemagne's coronation by the Pope in Rome on Christmas Day 800 effectively introduced it to the kingdoms of the former Western Roman Empire and English kings are regularly depicted wearing crowns from the 10th century.

In the late Middle Ages, these objects were important partly for their value and accrued in numbers within the Royal Treasury. The first page of the inventory of Richard II's treasure drawn up in 1398–99, for example, lists 11 gold crowns, collectively valued at the stupendous sum of £50,237. One of these, probably the possession of his Queen, Anne of Bohemia, survives.

For English kings, however, one crown associated with Edward the Confessor, from whom William the Conqueror claimed legitimate succession in 1066, acquired particular significance. The real date and history of St Edward's Crown—as it became known—are now beyond rescue and it seems to have changed in character within its documented history, being worn from the 14th century with an internal, fur-lined cap of estate and incorporating from the 15th century two intersecting arches of metal surmounted by a miniature orb and cross, a so-called 'imperial' form.

St Edward's Crown was used in the English coronation ceremony and became a mark of legitimacy. As with all the regalia, it was preserved in Westminster Abbey, where the shrine of this royal patronal saint stands. As a mark of its inalienable association with this church, it was exchanged for what was later termed the Crown of State when the King departed from the choir after the anointing ceremony.

St Edward's Crown survived the Reformation—when the coronation acquired a new significance by force of religious change—but it was destroyed after the Civil War.

In 1649, Oliver Cromwell may have dismissed England's royal regalia as 'worthless church stuffe', but he recognised its potent symbolism. His order that it be 'totallie broken and defaced' was followed by instructions to melt down all gold and silver items and remint the metal as coinage. The ancient crown of St Edward, valued by Cromwell's commissioners at £248 (and confusingly described as King Alfred's Crown), could not be allowed to survive as a reminder of erstwhile glories.

> ' It was at the moment the crown was placed on The King's head that his sovereignty was confirmed '

Within little more than a decade, a new regime reversed Cromwell's act of vandalism, castigated as 'the Rapine of the late unhappy times'. In May 1660, Charles II returned to England's throne; a meeting of his Coronation Committee in October commissioned a replacement for the medieval crown of Edward the Confessor. With four high arches, studded with jewels, topped by an orb and cross, and decorated with *fleur-de-lys* and crosses, Charles's new gold crown was symbolic proof of the return of royal government. 'When you appeare... shew your Selfe Gloryously to your People,' the Duke of Newcastle had implored the King.

The Committee commissioned not one, but two new crowns, one for the moment of crowning and a second for state occasions, such as the King's opening of Parliament. St Edward's Crown was placed on Charles's anointed head at the climax of his coronation, the greatest dramatic flourish of the ceremony. He wears it in a state portrait by John Michael Wright. In the painting, an armorial cloth of honour hangs behind the King, embroidered with an image of a crown that closely resembles Charles's own.

In 1661, the bill for new regalia came to an impressive £12,184 7s. 6d. Charles's government was on short rations and Robert Vyner, created royal goldsmith by letters patent in July 1661, would be driven to the brink of bankruptcy by late and incomplete payments over the following decade. To save money, Charles's new St Edward's Crown was decorated with borrowed jewels, at a cost of £500. This is how it appears in an unsigned painting of the royal regalia completed in the 1670s and the engraving included in Francis Sandford's pictorial record of the coronation of Charles's younger brother, James II, published in 1687. The jewels are modest in scale. Significantly, it was no longer stored at Westminster Abbey, but in the Tower of London, the royal stronghold within the walls of the capital.

The crown remained without permanent jewels until 1911. Then, on George V's instructions, it was set with the precious and semi-precious stones it retains, including nearly 350 rose-cut aquamarines, as well as tourmalines, rubies, amethysts and sapphires.

At Charles III's coronation, St Edward's Crown was placed upon The King's head after his anointing with holy oil. Although he became monarch on Elizabeth II's death on September 8, 2022, it was at that moment that his sovereignty was confirmed to the watching billions around the world. As the former Poet Laureate Carol Ann Duffy wrote in a poem celebrating the 60th anniversary of Elizabeth II's coronation in 2013: 'The Crown translates a woman to a Queen.'

A monarch crowned is a timeless image, remote from party politics, the squabbles or endeavours of any epoch, fleetingly shorn of his or her own virtues and shortcomings, →

A bright ring of power

Since the coronation of Edward VII in 1902, British sovereigns have worn a Coronation Ring made by royal goldsmiths Rundell, Bridge & Rundell in 1831. Created for William IV, it consists of an octagonal sapphire, surrounded by diamonds and overlaid with a ruby cross. William bequeathed his Coronation Ring to his widow, Queen Adelaide, who, in turn, bequeathed it to her niece, Queen Victoria. Victoria left both William and Adelaide's rings to the Crown, ending a tradition that coronation rings—made anew for each monarch—became part of the monarch's personal property.

Coronation rings are as old in origin as St Edward's Crown. A large sapphire today mounted in the Imperial State Crown may previously have formed the central stone of the Coronation Ring of Edward the Confessor, made in 1043.

The ring is traditionally placed on the monarch's fourth finger, as a symbol of his or her 'marriage' to their kingdom. Unlike Elizabeth I, who wore her Coronation Ring throughout her reign, Elizabeth II wore hers, like St Edward's Crown, only on the day. Her son laid his fingers on it to swear his oath.

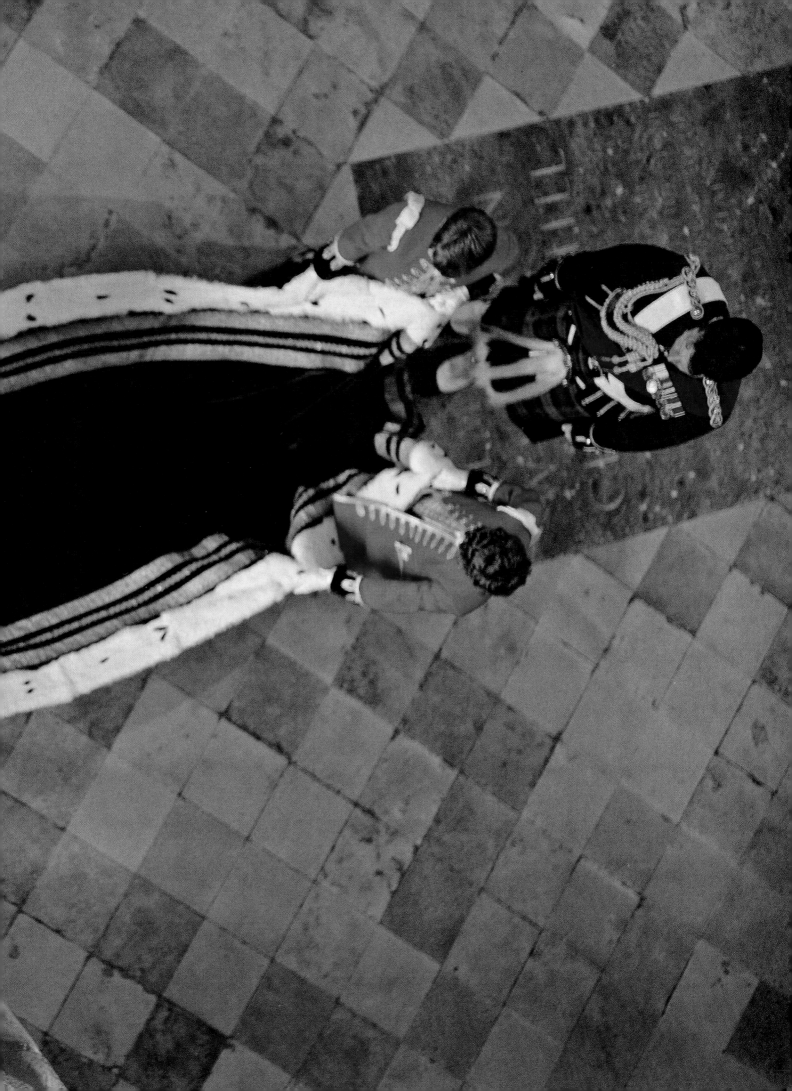

transformed into a glistering symbol of authority, of present trust and hopes for the future, shiningly branded by destiny, isolated in an age-old calling. At that moment, for the King himself, the congregation in Westminster Abbey and myriad spectators across the globe, time stood still. The King will carry that 4lb-weight with him for the remainder of his life, an imprint of a unique burden. It is a memory he will share with no one living.

Of the Imperial State Crown, which she wore annually for the State Opening of Parliament, Elizabeth II observed that it was meant to be heavy. That heaviness, like the crown itself, is a symbolic, as well as a physical weight. 'It hurt me a good deal,' Queen Victoria recalled of her own experience of wearing the crown, yet she remembered, too, as 'a most beautiful impressive moment', 'the Crown being placed on my head'.

' The Crown binds together sovereign, church and nation, past, present and future '

Images of early-Christian kings exploited the resemblance of crowns and halos. As a saint is God's servant, so the crowned sovereign is the servant of his subjects. A crown exacts more than it exalts. 'To be a king and wear a crown,' suggested Elizabeth I, 'is a thing more glorious to them that see it than it is pleasant to them that bear it.' The Archbishop's words at the pivotal moment—'God crown you with a crown of glory and righteousness' —are a reminder that, for its wearer, the crown is as much a symbol of aspiration and intent as of rank. In the liturgy of the coronation service, the sovereign attains 'the crown of an everlasting kingdom' through 'a right faith and manifold fruit of good works'.

For His Majesty, the symbolic crowning with St Edward's Crown, made for his namesake Charles II more than 350 years ago and last worn 70 years ago by his mother, places him in a continuum of these islands' rulers that stretches back 1,000 years. St Edward's Crown, used once in a reign, resembles the crown that 'shone with the various glitter of gold, silver and precious stones' at the coronation of the teenage Saxon king Eadwig in 955 or 956 or that of the Bible-clasping king in an illuminated manuscript in the collection of the British Library, which, produced some time after 966, is considered the earliest surviving depiction of a crowned king in England.

Although kingship pre-dates the fashioning of precious crowns, a crown has become

Above: **Charles II after his coronation in 1661, wearing the re-created St Edward's Crown.**
Facing page: **Charles III wears the same crown, which George V had set with jewels**

the defining emblem of royalty. The Crown, indeed, is the embodiment of the state, an entity that outlives kings and queens. For that reason, from the uniforms worn by policemen to postmen's vans, it is the image of the crown that, embroidered, emblazoned, engraved, painted and printed, asserts the authority of the state and articulates Britain's status as a constitutional monarchy.

For The King, the crown is also a link with his mother and, in time, his elder son. Neither he nor we have seen St Edward's Crown worn by anyone else and there are few people alive who remember the spectacle of a young Elizabeth II, enthroned and crowned to receive the homage of princes and peers.

Given his love of history, Charles III was undoubtedly reminded of ancient predecessors: Edgar, whose coronation in 973 His Majesty's will resemble in many essentials, or Edward the Confessor, who built the first Westminster Abbey and, in the first scene

of the Bayeux Tapestry, appears crowned and seated on a throne. The gold crown commissioned for Charles II in 1660 sought to re-create the crown first recorded as belonging to Edward, which, following his canonisation, acquired the status of a holy relic.

In December last year, Buckingham Palace announced the safe removal of St Edward's Crown from the Jewel House of the Tower of London as a preliminary to alter its size and fit ahead of the May coronation. The purpose of these alterations was to ensure His Majesty's comfort when wearing the crown. Yet comfort was not The King's chief concern. Shaped by historical precedent and the artistry of leading goldsmiths, ornamented with the sign of the Cross and studded with jewels acquired over more than 1,000 years, the Crown binds together sovereign, church and nation, past, present and future, in a gleaming golden circle without beginning or end, as heavy as expectation, as bright as hope. 👑

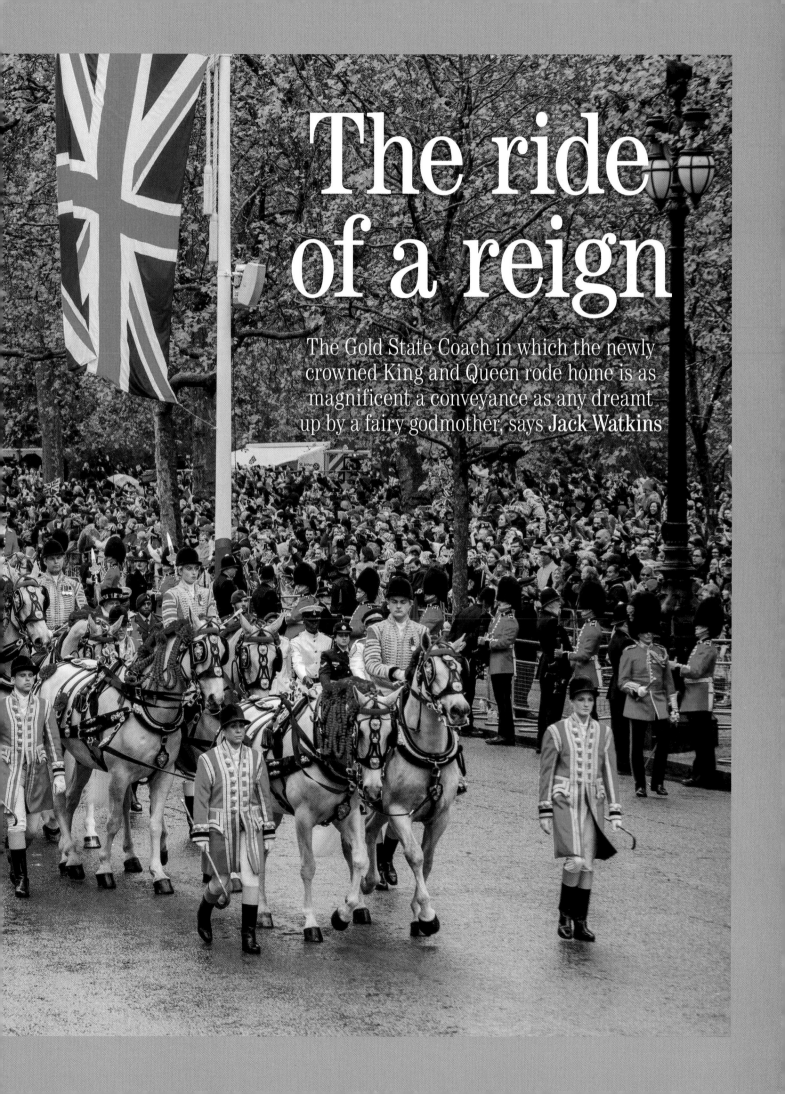

The ride of a reign

The Gold State Coach in which the newly
crowned King and Queen rode home is as
magnificent a conveyance as any dreamt
up by a fairy godmother, says **Jack Watkins**

Facing page: **With the Windsor Greys bedecked in blue for the occasion, the Gold State Coach processes along the Mall on May 6, 2023.** *Above:* **Footmen in Georgian garb**

FEW objects reflective of the fairy-tale allure and pageantry of the monarchy exert a greater visual impact at ground level than the Gold State Coach. Some of the most evocative images of Elizabeth II's reign include those of her being transported in this extravagantly gilded confection through London's streets as onlookers cheered.

Wheeled out for major ceremonial and state occasions, this remarkable and, by all accounts, remarkably uncomfortable conveyance was first used in 1762, when George III was driven in it to attend the State Opening of Parliament. People were so eager to see what it looked like, reported the *Daily Advertiser*, that 'several rooms in and near Parliament Street, are taken, at Two Guineas each, by Gentlemen and Ladies, to see His Majesty pass to the House in his new State Coach, which is thought to be the finest that was ever built'. Journalistic hyperbole aside, the glittering new carriage is unlikely to have disappointed the crowds.

It had been ordered by the young King soon after he succeeded his grandfather George II to the throne in 1760. The existing Baroque-styled State Coach, built for Queen Anne and later used by George I and George II, was looking distinctly passé, paling in comparison with the new coach of the Lord Mayor of London.

Although several designs were received, the project was handed to William Chambers, a rising star in royal circles at this time. He had been George's tutor in architecture,

when the latter was the Prince of Wales, and had designed the follies for the gardens at Kew Palace for the Dowager Princess Augusta.

According to Chambers's biographer John Harris (*Sir William Chambers: Knight of the Polar Star*), the full extent of the architect's involvement in the design is not known. However, the most finished version among the sketches to have survived was signed in 1760 by Chambers and Giovanni Battista Cipriani, the Florentine painter, draughtsman and designer who, as a friend of the architect, had been domiciled in England since 1755.

The sculptor Joseph Wilton, another of Chambers's associates, was asked to create a wax model of this drawing, and given responsibility for the carvings. Somewhat awkwardly, the task of building the carriage fell to Samuel Butler, the royal coachmaker, who had been involved with a rejected proposal submitted by his nephew, Mayfair cabinetmaker John Linnell.

The State Coach's decorations emphatically declare the glories of the British monarchy. Two tritons above the front wheels appear to be blowing conch shells to announce the arrival of the sovereign. Alongside eight gilded palm trees framing doors and windows, the cab ornamentation includes a symbol of the union of England, Scotland and Ireland on the roof in the form of three cherubs bearing the Imperial crown. Cipriani's seven painted panels include one at the front depicting an enthroned Britannia on the banks of the Thames being presented with laurels by Victory, with Religion, Justice, Valour, Fortitude,

> **' The decorations emphatically declare the glories of the monarchy '**

Royal role fulfilled: the coach, empty once more, is drawn home to the Royal Mews

Commerce and Plenty in attendance. The interior is lined with velvet and satin.

The carriage's immense weight has limited its suitability for anything other than the grandest of occasions. Yet, although it has been used at every coronation from George IV onwards, it has not been popular with its occupants. William IV, 'the Sailor King', likened it to a boat ride in rough seas. Victoria found it so uncomfortable she eventually refused to use it. George VI described his journey in it to his coronation as one of the most uncomfortable he'd ever had, a sentiment shared by Elizabeth II after hers. If our new King and Queen felt the same, they showed no sign. ❧

Gilt-edged facts

The Gold State Coach, first used in 1762, is the third-oldest surviving coach in Britain, behind the Speaker's State Coach and the Lord Mayor of London's Coach (1758)

It was such an unseasonably wet, cold day for the coronation of Elizabeth II on June 2, 1953, that Royal Mews staff reportedly strapped a hot-water bottle under the seat for the young Queen. It rained again for Charles III's parade

Made of giltwood (400 books of gold leaf cover the wood), it is only for the use of the Sovereign. In the Platinum Jubilee pageant, a holographic image of the Queen was used

Weighing four tons, the coach is drawn by eight Windsor Greys, with postilions riding the near-side horses, and never travels above walking pace. **On May 6, 2023, head coachman was Matthew Powers and the horses were Icon, Shadow, Milford Haven, Newark, Echo, Knightsbridge, Meg and Tyrone**

The gilded crown on the top was carved from timbers taken from HMS *Victory* and the internal handrails from RY *Britannia*

The interior includes pieces from Caernarfon Castle, Canterbury Cathedral, 10 Downing Street, Henry VIII's flagship *Mary Rose* and the Antarctic bases of Capt Scott and Sir Ernest Shackleton

A rapturous welcome

The weather couldn't suppress the nation's
joy at the crowning of our new King

The home stretch: the Coronation Procession, with The King and Queen and Royal Family members at the rear, heads down the Mall

Dressed in the uniform of the Colonel of the Blues and Royals, The King's sister is also Gold Stick-in-Waiting

Princess Charlotte wears a headpiece by Jess Collett in collaboration with Alexander McQueen, as Prince Louis smiles at the crowds

The Queen's necklace was made by Garrard for Victoria in 1858

The Princess of Wales looks radiant in a laurel diadem that matches her daughter's and The Duke of Edinburgh waves at the camera

In the 39 acres of the largest private garden in London, The King and Queen receive the Royal Salute from 4,000 military service-men and women (and one dog). Behind the serried ranks, the massed pipes and drums of 18 regiments provided musical accompaniment ♔

The man who is King

The breadth of Charles III's interests and influence
is as impressive as the compassion he feels for people
from all walks of life, as four friends of COUNTRY LIFE,
who know and have worked with The King, reveal

Greeting Sir John Major in 2019. Scrupulously outside politics, yet respected by politicians, The King's voice is worth listening to

All hail The King

Sir John Major makes his tribute to a man of empathy and many interests

NO monarch of our nation has been better prepared than Charles III. He has moved into the role with a sure touch and a deep understanding of all that will be required of him. I do not claim to be an intimate of The King—and nor should any politician—but I know enough to be confident that he will become a very successful monarch and a much-loved one, too.

The nexus between the monarch and the Government is a sensitive one. It can easily be misunderstood and more easily misinterpreted. The monarch has every right to be fully informed about the actions and intentions of the Government, not least because each and every one of them will have an impact on the lives of those he or she serves.

Some critics have complained that—when still Prince of Wales—The King 'lobbied' ministers too forcefully; but, in my experience, such a criticism is woefully misguided. During the years I was Prime Minister, we met to discuss a wide range of issues and I found the meetings to be hugely beneficial. Yes, I was

questioned about policy. And, yes, opinions were expressed. Yet I was never put under any pressure to follow any particular course.

The Prince invariably put his concerns to me fully and fairly—as I believe it was his duty to do—but I have never known him, or any other senior member of the Royal Family,

> ' The King saw his mother's dedication all her life. He will be no less diligent '

step over the accepted line between Crown and Government. The question, as I saw it, was straightforward. Would I prefer an heir to the throne who highlighted a legitimate concern about what is happening in our country or one who showed no interest in how our people live and the problems they face? The answer to me was clear.

As monarch, there is no doubt The King will be circumspect, but I hope not too much

so. I know of no prime minister who did not find the late Queen's private counsel of immense value and that will hold true for Charles III as well. The King has a personal gift of empathy and an understanding of hardship. Both are sharpened by an acute sensitivity to others. It is that sensitivity that underpins his ability to sympathise with the ambitions, the hopes and the fears of people from all backgrounds. To be able to do so is a great strength for anyone in public life— and most especially in a monarch.

He has a talent for putting people at ease and, as did the late Queen, knows far more about how his people live than anyone— other than those close to him—might realise. From early childhood, The King was immersed in a world that put duty to others before self. He saw his mother's own dedication until the very end of her life. He will be no less diligent.

A modern man, he has often been well ahead of public opinion: on the encouragement of the young; on compassionate capitalism; on religious tolerance; on the built and natural environment; on agriculture; on climate change; and on so much more besides.

Often, The King was so far ahead of received wisdom that he had to wait for it to catch up, which generally—albeit slowly—it did. Ideas he advocated that once were mocked have become orthodoxy.

The point is this: he leads opinion and does not follow it—nor is he influenced by fashionable chatter, for he has too much of his parents' good common sense to do that.

I hope The King will continue to talk—publicly as appropriate and privately when necessary—of the importance of community; of the natural world; of Nature; of compassion and caring; of his Armed Forces; and of his work for so many good causes. He should not be silent on issues that have been lifetime passions and upon which he is an authority.

Away from his duties, The King will still, I hope, find time for his private pursuits. His love of painting is known, but he also enjoys the theatre, notably Shakespeare. He loves listening to music—from classical to modern —and has an infectious sense of the absurd: it is no surprise that Monty Python films and *Blackadder* are among his comedies of choice.

Yet, perhaps, The King's greatest passion remains that of creating gardens. His weekends at Highgrove and Birkhall were spent designing, landscaping, digging, planting and weeding—he does much of the physical work himself. No doubt, the gardens at Windsor, Balmoral and Sandringham will now receive equal attention. He will not waste his days of leisure. The King is a man with hobbies and interests aplenty, which is why he so easily finds a connection with all those he meets.

In a country and nation changing faster than is comfortable, The King knows our monarchy must continue to evolve. For centuries, there was a mystique around the Royal Family; but, over recent decades, public interest and modern media has pulled the curtain aside.

Today, nearly every aspect of their lives is public property and nowhere is this searchlight more probing than upon The King and his immediate family. On any human level, this is intrusive and, at times, must be deeply upsetting, but The King carries the burden with dignity and fortitude.

Charles III is a man who believes in evolution, not revolution, cares about the common good and will seek to heal, not divide. In troubled times, we are fortunate to have such a monarch.

On May 6, we moved seamlessly from the Elizabethan to the Carolean age. As tradition dictated, bells rang out and people everywhere proclaimed 'God Save The King'.

From what we have seen thus far, I believe that proclamation was not merely out of respect, but out of genuine affection for His Majesty, King Charles III. Long may he reign.
Sir John Major KG CH was Prime Minister of the UK from November 1990 to May 1997

A lone voice in the architectural wilderness

Simon Jenkins pays respect to the fearless way The King has stood up for his beliefs

THE Prince of Wales was a man of many opinions. Some he kept to himself; others were mildly eccentric. But, on one subject, he made no attempt to conceal or restrain them: architecture. On this most public of art forms, he was unashamedly controversial. From the style of buildings to the nuances of town planning, he knew what he thought and would gladly take on any opponent, constitutional convention be damned.

He first broke cover in a speech in 1984. Still in his thirties, he had already declared his radicalism on alternative medicine, organic agriculture and community volunteering. Then came an invitation to speak on the 150th anniversary of the Royal Institute of British Architects at Hampton Court, an irresistible platform for his views on prevailing modernism. He tore up briefing notes and platitudes sent to guide him and disregarded pleas from aides who had wind of what he might say.

He duly launched a full-frontal attack on the profession there arrayed before him. Architects had, he said, 'consistently ignored the feelings and wishes of the mass of ordinary people in this country'. They were trained to do one thing, 'tear down and rebuild… for the approval of fellow architects, not for tenants'. He savaged their defiling of London, 'once with one of the most beautiful skylines of any great city'. St Paul's was to be 'dwarfed by yet another giant glass stump better suited to downtown Chicago'. To the west, the National Gallery extension was 'a vast municipal fire station… a monstrous carbuncle on the face of a much-loved and elegant friend'.

The dinner dissolved into near chaos. The guest of honour, the architect Charles Correa, refused to give his own speech. The National Gallery's architect, Peter Ahrends, said the Prince's views were 'offensive, reactionary and ill-considered'. Norman Foster fumed and Richard Rogers complained the Royal Family 'did not practise what they preached'. Yet press and public reaction sounded a different →

London's skyline might look very different without The King

Playing to a handicap of four goals, The King ruled the polo field in his day

note. The reaction was overwhelmingly favourable. The Prince was no longer murmuring to plants, but talking robust common sense. Glass tower and carbuncle bit the dust.

In many of his controversies, Charles III tended to lapse into worthy abstractions. Not so in architecture. He, indeed, practised his preaching. In 1987, he again took the stage, to attack the City's plan to replace the bleak post-war rebuilding of Paternoster Square north of St Paul's with another 'desecration' of toxic Modernism. He compared the City fathers unfavourably with the Luftwaffe, which knocked down buildings 'but didn't replace them with anything more offensive than rubble'. He offered a plan of his own, drawn up by the neo-Classicist architect John Simpson. It was adopted and more or less built.

The Prince then turned to his own Duchy of Cornwall land outside Dorchester in Dorset, where he invited the favoured Léon Krier to build a completely new town. Traditional in both layout and design, Poundbury took some eight years of argument and near failure to get off the ground. The Prince never gave up. Still detested by Modernists, the estate has matured into a traditional mix of Cheltenham and Chipping Campden, its houses and flats hotly in demand. As if to rub salt into detractors' wounds, in 1992, the Prince launched his Institute for Architecture in Regent's Park. Together with other similar bodies, it morphed into The Prince's Foundation, ardently committed to teaching the skills required for Classical and vernacular architecture.

Throughout his interventions, the Prince was adamant that he was doing no more than any private citizen in expressing an opinion and displaying his taste. He galvanised support for the lobbyists of SAVE Britain's Heritage in rescuing Wentworth Woodhouse in South Yorkshire and in fundraising to restore Dumfries House in Ayrshire. He would protest that he had no more power than the 'opinion-formers' who criticised him, a little naïve. He was ruthless in stopping a Brutalist replacement for Chelsea Barracks by intervening with its owners, the Qatari royal family.

> ‘ **The King's subjects would be sorry if he was over-curtailed by convention** ’

The King's most controversial technique was during the Blair Government, whose ministers he bombarded with scribbled 'black-spider' letters on anything that stirred his dismay. His attention span was notoriously short and the memos, when revealed under court order in 2015, were outspoken on topics ranging from military supplies to badger culls. As president of the National Trust, he once asked me as its chairman what we should do about the situation in Darfur. I had to explain that we had few members there. His concern was sincere, his application less so.

On architecture, one thing that stood The King in good stead was the fact that public opinion was on his side. After his Paternoster speech, he received some 2,000 letters, almost all in approval. When Modernist architects, including Rogers, Zaha Hadid and Lord Foster, declared his interventions 'an abuse of power... and of democratic planning', the press had only to look at their letters pages.

He was aware that his opinions would have to be restrained when he became monarch. A Shakespeare fan, he knew Prince Hal's warning on becoming Henry V: 'Presume not that I am the thing I was... I have turned away my former self.' His private secretary Sir Michael Peat said he was scrupulous of the need to 'ensure he [was] not politically contentious or party political'. His campaigns as Prince were time limited and he wanted to fufil them.

The political establishment was plainly irritated to have a black spider crawling over its decisions. Equally, I sense that a large—albeit always mercurial—majority of The King's subjects would be sorry if he was over-curtailed by constitutional convention. His was a lonely voice. Architects had long bullied politicians and planners into a partial view of how modern Britain should look.

For a public figure to give voice to a contrary opinion was thoroughly worthwhile. It would be sad to see it go.
Author and columnist Simon Jenkins FSA FRSL was editor of the 'Evening Standard' from 1976–78 and 'The Times' from 1990–92. He chaired the National Trust in 2008–14

'He's already changed the world'

Tony Juniper salutes a man far ahead of his time

FEW of us these days are unaware of the momentous environmental challenges facing our world. Global heating, mass extinction of species, ecosystem degradation and the depletion of resources from fish stocks to soils are regularly in the news. It was not always like this, with such questions relegated to the margins of society's concerns for decades. That they are now on the agenda and mainstream is down to the work of visionary individuals who could see the need for change. Most prominent among them has been the former Prince of Wales, now Charles III.

Long before celebrities drove Teslas and Greenpeace was a household name, in the days when organic agriculture was a fringe pursuit and few people had heard of the ozone layer, never mind climate change, there were very few voices speaking out for our planet's future.

It took a lot of courage to stand up and say what was happening, especially at a time when doing so often attracted ridicule. Back in December 1968, however, that is exactly what the 20-year-old Prince did, delivering his first environmental speech, at a conference about the future of the countryside in Wales.

It was the beginning of the most outstanding contribution on environmental issues from anyone anywhere in the world. When he was Prince of Wales, The King shone a bright light on pretty much every environmental question. His initiatives have raised the profile of tropical rainforests, the existential threat of climate change, the impact of excessive pesticide use, the need to protect food security through regenerative farming, the plight of the oceans and the opportunities arising from moves to sustainable fishing.

His advocacy has been based on advice from world experts, but also on seeing for himself the questions at first hand, reading vast quantities of material and participating in discussions, briefings and round tables. The breadth of his knowledge is as wide as the subjects upon which he has sought to galvanise action. In making progress, he has convened groups of influencers at the highest levels, including major global companies, governments, significant non-governmental groups and leading scientific bodies to find consensus on complex challenges, such as halting tropical deforestation. The initiative he originated on that subject, The Prince's Rainforests Project (and the International Sustainability Unit that followed it) was influential in achieving significant outcomes, including at the Paris Climate Change →

With the blessing of Nature: The King has long worked to help the natural world and the people who live therein

Summit in 2015, which reached a breakthrough agreement that remains today.

His environmental work has, of course, been accompanied by interests and contributions in other areas, including education, health and architecture. Although, for some, this created the impression of a man who jumped from one issue to another, with a focus on buildings in the morning and farming in the afternoon, his 2010 book *Harmony* brought it all together. It revealed a golden thread that ran through it all, a unifying philosophy with Nature as being at the heart of human wellbeing and how the circular economy of the natural world must inspire the future of the human world.

He has helped multiple charities through being their patron, as well as setting up dozens of his own, including The Prince's Trust and

Business in the Community. Whereas some environmental advocates see people as the problem, he has always regarded them as the solution. His calls for sustainable farming centre as much on farmers as on soils, water and pollinators. His work for sustainable fishing has been much about fishing communities and his efforts to save the dwindling tropical rainforests embraced the future of the people who live there and from whose cultures came ideas that inspired aspects of *Harmony*.

He worked in a tricky space for more than five decades, raising issues and making progress by bringing people together to forge solutions. He used his position with great skill and dedication, to great effect. Above the fray and with no axe of vested interest to grind, he fostered collaboration. He didn't

have to do what he did, but his personal calling was to make a difference and that is what he set out to do. Now, his challenge is to find an accommodation between his mission to make progress on the most important issues facing our world and the constitutional requirements of being head of state.

Since becoming King, he has already demonstrated something of what he can do, working with the Government to host two receptions at Buckingham Palace, bringing leaders together to encourage action. The first was in October 2022, just before the COP27 climate-change meeting in Sharm El Sheikh. The other took place in February, adding momentum in the wake of the successful Nature summit in Montreal at the end of last year. Although his personal voice will necessarily now be less

Cometh the hour, cometh The King

Dame Fiona Reynolds praises a dedicated monarch with the personal touch

A KING who warned of the carbon and Nature crises years before the rest of the world woke up to them. A King who is as comfortable in a farmhouse kitchen, a shepherd's crook by his side, as in a royal palace. A King whose hands are scarred with the toil of hedge-laying, yet soft enough to enfold those who have received public awards, from knights and dames to recipients of British Empire Medals. A King who has helped countless young people take hold of their future, at the same time as persuading some of the world's largest businesses to embrace sustainability. A King who loves nothing better than a quiet hour in a beautiful garden, where he impresses the local expert with his horticultural knowledge. And a King with a fine eye for architecture and design, from the vernacular to the unashamedly grand. In short: a King with a keen sense of beauty and how fundamental it is to our lives.

> ' He is always there, quiet, compassionate and genuine '

In this time of contested priorities and short-term politics, isn't this exactly the kind of King we need? When public policy seems ill-equipped to deal with a pressured economy and successive crises, our King understands the bigger picture and has an unerring instinct for what motivates and sustains the people of the UK.

He knows our country intimately and understands it better than most. He has visited every corner of the British Isles, taking time to acquaint himself with the spirit of each place and bringing delight as a royal visitor, even privately at National Trust properties. And he remembers: people, details, dates and stories. Years later, in a conversation about something entirely different, The King might draw an analogy or remember an anecdote that can only have come from such a fleeting, but clearly meaningful experience.

He cares. The joy of out-of-the-limelight visits to the Lake District—a landscape he loves—were jolted into another dimension by the horrors of foot-and-mouth disease in 2001. He cheered us on as we did all we could to save the Herdwick sheep from destruction from contiguous culling (today's flocks are direct descendants of those shepherded by Beatrix Potter). As the restrictions were lifted, he was among the first to visit the farms and their occupants who had been so terribly afflicted by the disease. He did the same in so many contexts: after floods and disasters he was always there, quiet, compassionate and genuine, understanding what people needed; not grandstanding, but offering real empathy, drawn from his own insights into the realities of people's lives.

In *Harmony*, perhaps The King's most personal articulation of his credo, he wrote: 'This book offers inspiration for those who feel, deep down, that there is a more balanced way of looking at the world, and more harmonious ways of living.' If that was true in 2010, it is more than ever now, as the implications of our failure to control the speed of climate change or reverse the decline of Nature have become ever more apparent.

Our world, our country and the places we live in and love are ecosystems of interconnected networks, underpinned by Nature and natural resources, but heavily influenced by humans. As the Dasgupta review into the economics of Nature showed us, human activity started to outstrip its ability to regenerate in the 1950s. The world is a tapestry of woven threads, which are now beginning to break.

Our King may rarely speak publicly on these issues now, as he did in the past, but make no mistake, we have already heard what he has to say. If ever we needed a role model to lead us to a better, more sustainable future, it is there in the form of our King, Charles III. 🌿
Dame Fiona Reynolds was formerly Master of Emmanuel College, Cambridge, and director-general of the National Trust. She is now the chair of Governors at the Royal Agricultural University, Cirencester, and the author of 'The Fight for Beauty'

prominent, these kinds of convening events are evidently compatible with his position as sovereign and more will follow.

Whatever the future may hold, however, our King has already changed the world, creating a legacy that historians will undoubtedly judge as going far beyond what might have been expected from the positions into which he happened to be born. If we do succeed in avoiding an ecological disaster later this century, part of the reason will be because of what he did for 50 years and more, driving a renaissance in ideas, raising awareness, bringing people together, celebrating good practice and supporting those who, like him, sought to make a difference.
Tony Juniper is an environmentalist, writer and the chair of Natural England

Words of wisdom

The King has inspired people from across many fields of enterprise, from architecture to acting, with his words and actions. **Amie Elizabeth White** listens to what he and his admirers have to say

'He has an overwhelming sense of energy, a relentless feeling of wanting to get things done, to exercise change for the better'

Ben Pentreath, architectural designer for the Duchy of Cornwall →

'I learned the way a monkey learns—by watching its parents'

The King

'I think that's one thing you notice when you're with King Charles: his company. It doesn't matter what walk of life you're from, what age you are, he finds a common ground, and makes you feel that you deserve to be there'

Luke Evans, actor →

'Prince Charles is definitely my hero; he uses his position to do only good in this world'

Dame Vivienne Westwood, fashion designer →

'If we care about the health of our rural landscapes and communities, we must provide encouragement and support to those who are toiling away at their core'

The King, COUNTRY LIFE Leader, 2020

'He continues to astound me with his simple, yet profound observations born out of experience and intuition. He believes that we are not separate from Nature, we are Nature, and that we cannot separate who we are from what we do'

← Patrick Holden, co-founder of the Sustainable Food Trust

'I want to try and leave something better behind than I found. We need to make sure that we look after the countryside and our environment in a way that doesn't prejudice our grandchildren's chances. This is really what lies behind what is now described as sustainable development'

The King

'It's not throwing money at a problem, it's throwing intelligence and care and affection, and I think at the centre of it is [His Majesty's] profound affection for what he does and the people for whom he does it'

↑ Sir Ben Kingsley, actor

→

'When The King gave a powerful speech on climate change at the Pyramids… I thought back to those views, glad to know that our fragile planet has such a friend'

Tim Scott Bolton,
Royal Tour artist and author
of *A Brush with Rivers*, on a royal
tour of Jordan and Egypt in 2021

'I have an image of what a British gentleman looks like, and that image finds real expression in Prince Charles. He is beyond fashion— he is an archetype of style'

Donatella Versace,
fashion designer →

'I feel more than anything else it's my duty to worry about everybody and their lives in this country, to try to find a way of improving things if I possibly can'

The King

'[Highgrove is] the passion project of arguably the best royal gardener in history… if you want to look into the heart of the future King of England, then look no further than his private garden'

Alan Titchmarsh, author and gardener →

'The Prince's Trust is not an arm's-length organisation for my father; he cares deeply about [it] because it is a living projection of his values'

The Prince of Wales →

'On my frequent visits to different rural communities, I am always struck by the resilience, good humour and positive attitudes of the people who live and work there. I am certain they can make the huge and far reaching changes that are required, once the right framework has been established, while maintaining the very special character that makes our countryside so special'

The King, COUNTRY LIFE Leader, 2019

'We copied our hairstyle from Prince Charles, not the Beatles'

← Dave Clark (*seated*), musician

'I find myself born into this particular position. I'm determined to make the most of it. And to do whatever I can to help. And I hope I leave things behind a little bit better than I found them'

The King

'If the life of the land teaches anything, it is the need to look at the long term; at the deep and enduring strengths and qualities that continue through the slow rhythm of the seasons, through Nature's ever-rejuvenating generation of new life. We must respect the temporary fury of the waves, but we can trust the steady character of the tides. We must judge by the season, not the storm'

The King, COUNTRY LIFE Leader, 2020

Saluting our new Queen

Reading to children, rescuing dogs or campaigning to end domestic abuse, our newly crowned Queen attracts admiration and devotion in all she meets, says **Jane Wheatley**

THERE was once a little girl called Camilla, whose father read stories to his children every night, instilling in her an enduring love of books and the imaginative adventures they promised. He did all of us a great favour, because, when his daughter grew up and married the man who became King, she determined that all children should have the opportunity to lose themselves in a good story.

Soon after she became Duchess of Cornwall and assumed her role as a working royal, the author Michael Morpurgo was invited to Buckingham Palace to talk about literature for children and what the Duchess could do to help. 'It was quite early on when she first appeared on the scene and she was mightily sincere about it,' he recalls. 'She was very authentic and clearly understood the importance of libraries and books for children.' They went on to meet often, even sitting together in a tent at the Hay Festival in Wales to read stories to assembled children.

> **She shares books she loves with children and adults, "raising the flag for literature"**

As The Queen, she has her own charity and Instagram account, The Queen's Reading Room, sharing books she loves with children and adults around the world and recruiting well-known actors and authors, including Sir Michael, to give readings and recommendations. 'She is raising the flag for literature,' he enthuses. 'I don't think any member of the Royal Family has been so involved in the culture of the country since Prince Albert.'

In 2010, to celebrate the 15th anniversary of the Women's Prize for Fiction, its founder, novelist Kate Mosse, asked the then Duchess of Cornwall to present the awards. 'People had told me she was a big reader, who was interested in women and girls writing, and

Facing page: **Taking her place on the balcony.** *Above:* **Mutual support: The King and Queen**

we needed someone of her stature to mark the moment,' remembers Mrs Mosse. 'Back then, she was still a controversial figure and objections came from people who had never met her, but we stuck to our guns.' Of the rough times the former Mrs Parker Bowles had to face, Mrs Mosse observes: 'She has weathered it all with great dignity and grace. It doesn't matter who you are, women being silenced is common to everybody and I admire how she has ploughed her own furrow.'

Since her marriage in 2005, The Queen has taken on a full calendar of royal duties, but much of her work and interests has developed under the radar, following up with people she's met and often bringing them together informally. After an undercover visit to a rape crisis centre in 2009, she held a reception at Clarence House, inviting people involved in the field of combating sexual violence from the Home Secretary downwards, many of whom had never met before. It's what she does →

best, linking people up and making common cause. As one charity boss told me: 'She is so much more than a name over the door.'

'People go away feeling really respected and feel the warmth of her personality,' Jude Kelly, founder of the Women of the World (WOW) Foundation, told royal biographer Penny Junor. 'She's lived her life, some of it in public, and that's got a deeply painful aspect to it— she's obviously transferred her difficulties into a greater compassion for others.'

In 2016, The Duchess visited the charity SafeLives—which helps survivors of domestic abuse—and met Diana Parkes, whose daughter Joanna had been murdered by her estranged husband. Visibly appalled by the stories she heard, she became a staunch ally of the charity and patron in 2020. Last year, she told Emma Barnett on BBC Radio Four's *Woman's Hour* how deeply shocked she had been by what she had learnt at that first meeting: 'I don't think in those days I knew much about domestic abuse,' she admitted. 'It was a very hush-hush subject, taboo. It's talked about much more now.' She had 'zoned in' suggested Mrs Barnett: 'Quite correct,' nodded The Duchess. 'I shan't let go now. I hope I shall be doing [this work] for a lifetime.'

> ' As The King once said of her, "she's the best listener in the world" '

Traditionally, on overseas trips, members of the Royal Family might go to the ballet, view a military parade or attend a remembrance service; The Queen likes to pop into a women's refuge. From Bahrain to Lagos, wherever possible, she will seek out survivors of domestic violence or sexual assault and hear their stories, raising the profile of each service and its needs. As The King once said of her, 'she's the best listener in the world'.

In Rwanda, she gave the keynote speech at a conference on violence against women and girls before talking to children at Kigali public library, stocked with books sent from Book Aid International, of which she is patron.

These two causes are among 100 patronages and presidencies she has taken on. Some were inherited from her mother-in-law, the late Queen, including Battersea Dogs & Cats Home—she has two Jack Russells, Beth and Bluebell, that were rescued by the charity— where she met the late comedian and fellow dog lover Paul O'Grady. 'We hit it off straight away,' he told me. 'I met the Queen many

At the heart of the realm: the new Queen awaits the weight of Queen Mary's Crown

times and used to get a bit nervous, but with the new Queen it's different, like meeting an old friend; I don't want to sound presumptuous, but she's so approachable. And she's so good for The King, the two of them together, that should have happened years ago.

'She was a pariah at one stage; I think she survived it so well because she's very true to herself. As me Mum used to say, "a steady hand is needed to steer through stormy seas".'

Soon after the late Queen said it was her 'sincere wish' that Camilla should be known as Queen Consort when Charles became King, she became a Royal Lady of the Most Noble Order of the Garter, the highest order of chivalry and even made the pages of *Vogue*.

When the team arrived for the shoot, she said: 'Sorry you've got to photograph an old bat this morning,' adding, looking regretfully at her hands: 'I did have some nails, but I lost them all gardening yesterday.' The photographer snapped away, calling out 'beautiful, ma'am' and making her chuckle. As someone once said of her: 'She has a deep and infectious laugh and often seems to be the one having the most fun in the room.'

Helena Kennedy has known The Queen since before her marriage, when Baroness Kennedy was chair of the British Council and spent a weekend at Sandringham: 'We talked about an Anne Tyler novel we had both read and I realised she was a real book person. When I chaired the Booker Prize, I asked her to present the award... we would send her the final six, she had always read them and was always keen to meet the writers.'

As do many, Baroness Kennedy admits she is a big fan of The Queen: 'She is down to earth, human, compassionate and a great champion of women's rights. I did an interview in *The Sunday Times*, in which I said I desperately needed help chartering planes [for evacuating women lawyers out of Afghanistan]. The next day, her office got in touch to say: "The Queen Consort would like to make a donation." Later, she suggested that I bring some of them to Clarence House for tea. I brought three judges. She was wonderful, they all adore her.'

Similarly, during the pandemic, Sir Michael spoke on Radio 4 about his local pub in Devon putting on a weekly three-course lunch for isolated elderly people in the community. 'The next day, I got a call from Clarence House, saying: "The Duchess would like to come and have lunch with your OAPs."' Was he surprised? 'Well, yes, a bit; but I said I would arrange it.'

The lunch was delayed by lockdowns, but the royal couple remembered the engagement and 'drove to deepest Devon and spent an hour and a half there. It was a private visit; there was no press and no one made anything of it'.

She may have shone when she was crowned alongside her husband, but under the radar is where our new Queen truly likes to be. 🌿

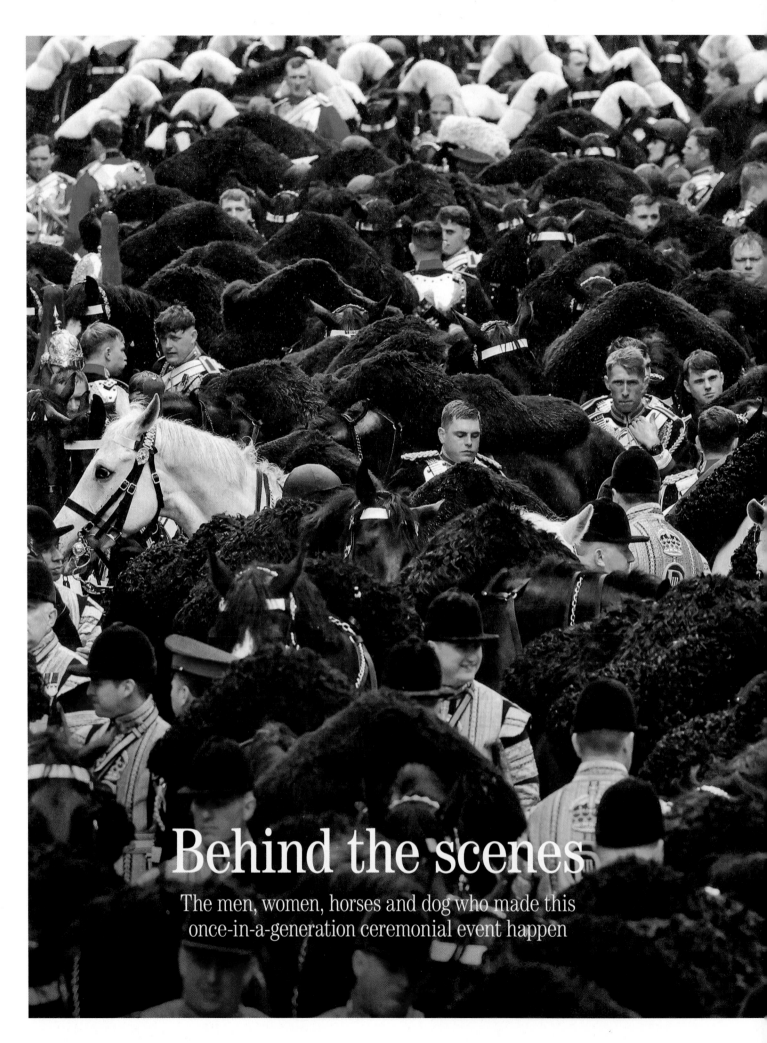

Behind the scenes

The men, women, horses and dog who made this
once-in-a-generation ceremonial event happen

Servicemen, women and horses of the Household Division and staff of the Royal Mews take a well-earned break after weeks of preparation

Top and right: **Fighting the commute, not the French—soldiers travel to London Waterloo ahead of the ceremony.** *Above:* **Coronation-themed treats, featuring the Imperial State Crown, are prepared by the Biscuiteers Baking Company**

Above right: **The new Royal Cypher takes pride of place on the uniforms of Royal Mews staff.** *Right:* **'There's no such thing as bad weather, only unsuitable clothing'. The umbrella party awaits the arrival of service guests at the Great West Door of Westminster Abbey**

The badge of The King's Watermen. Some 24 remain under the command of The King's Bargemaster

Tottenham-based Kashket & Partners made the red wool tunic for Seamus (Turlough Mor), the Irish Guards' Irish wolfhound mascot. He wears a solid silver dog collar worn by the regiment's first mascot, Brian Beru, which is engraved with the names of all the canine mascots that preceded him

A member of the Royal School of Needlework painstakingly stitches on the coat of arms of The Queen on Her Majesty's Throne Chair ahead of the ceremony. The arms were granted to her by Elizabeth II after Camilla's marriage to the then Prince of Wales in 2005

Above: **Turning up to turn out: members of the Royal Signal Corps adjust their caps, which feature the winged messenger Mercury.** *Left:* **A trooper of the Lifeguards prepares his Albert Helmet and white plume, traditionally composed of horse hair. The helmets are made by the Birmingham-based company Firmin & Sons, who have been the armourers for every British monarch since Charles II** ♛

Greeting the nation

The newly crowned King and Queen make their first appearance on the iconic balcony of Buckingham Palace

Left to right: **The Duke of Edinburgh, the Earl of Wessex, Lady Louise Windsor, Vice-Admiral Sir Tim Laurence, The Duchess of Edinburgh, Princess Charlotte, The Princess Royal, The Princess of Wales, Prince Louis, The Prince of Wales, The King's Pages of Honour (Ralph Tollemache, Prince George, Lord Oliver Cholmondeley and Nicholas Barclay), King Charles III and Queen Camilla, The Queen's Pages of Honour (Louis and Gus Lopes, Freddy Parker Bowles and Arthur Elliot), Ladies in Attendance Annabel Elliot and the Marchioness of Lansdowne, Princess Alexandra of Kent, The Duke of Kent, The Duchess of Gloucester and The Duke of Gloucester**

Unfazed by the occasion, Prince Louis makes sure his voice is heard above the cheers of the crowds, much to his family's amusement

The King's Pages of Honour (*left to right*): Ralph Tollemache, 12, son of The King's godson, Edward Tollemache; Prince George, nine, second in line to the throne; Lord Oliver Cholmondeley, 13, son of the 7th Marquess of Cholmondeley, The King's Lord-in Waiting; and Nicholas Barclay, 13, grandson of Sarah Troughton, Lord-Lieutenant of Wiltshire and a close friend of Queen Camilla's

The Red Arrows roar along the length of The Mall, delighting the public and royals alike. Despite having performed more than 4,800 displays in 57 countries worldwide, this has been the most important assignment for the nine-strong team and its BAE Hawk jets

The King and Queen make their first appearance on the balcony of Buckingham Palace after returning from Westminster Abbey. Hundreds of thousands of well-wishers lined the Mall, some waiting for days, to witness the magnificent spectacle 🜲

Dishes fit for The King

John Williams, executive chef at The Ritz in London, talks to **Emma Hughes** about good game cookery and creating The King's favourite recipe, pheasant crumble pie. Plus, the Coronation Quiche

Photographs by John Carey

Facing page: **Game maestro John Williams has cooked at The Ritz since 2004 and led the restaurant to its first Michelin star in 2017.** *Above:* **Sustainable and delicious: pheasant crumble pie is true British bounty**

FOR John Williams, it began with a bag of grouse. 'I'd just been taken on as an apprentice at The Percy Arms in Northumberland and they wanted me to pluck and gut them,' The Ritz's executive chef remembers, sitting in his office before the lunch service begins.

'It was the first thing I had ever touched in a professional kitchen. I come from a seaside town, so I was much more used to fish and I'd definitely never encountered that aroma before,' he divulges with a smile. 'But, you know, today, it's one of my favourite smells. Come the Glorious Twelfth, I'm outside that door anxiously waiting for the birds to arrive.'

Towering above Piccadilly, the setting of The Ritz is as metropolitan as it gets, yet its restaurant menu is a hymn to the British countryside's bounty. Every autumn, game reigns supreme in the Michelin-starred dining room, from grouse with all the traditional accompaniments to Norfolk quail with sweetcorn and verjus. Venison wellington is a celebrated choice, together with the likes of sika deer with red cabbage, juniper and Cumberland sauce.

With game catching the eye of a new generation of young, urban diners—restaurants such as St John and The Quality Chop House routinely sell out of snipe, woodcock and hare in season and a search on Instagram for #grouse brings up 214,000 hits—Mr Williams was well and truly ahead of the curve.

'I think it went out of favour for a while because chefs weren't handling it correctly,' he says. 'People used to tell me "I like my game green, man—it's got →

Pheasant crumble pie recipe

INGREDIENTS

For the stock
1 pheasant

1 medium onion, cut into a medium dice

1 large carrot, cut into a large dice

4 sticks of celery, cut into quarters

2 bay leaves

Large sprig of thyme

6 juniper berries

4 peppercorns

Splash of sherry

For the roux sauce
40g butter

40g plain flour

290ml pheasant stock

Dash of cream

Chopped parsley and thyme

Seasoning

For the crumble
170g butter

56g white breadcrumbs

28g finely grated Parmesan

2 smoked streaky-bacon rashers

METHOD

> To make the stock, place the whole pheasant in a large saucepan and cover with water. Add all the other ingredients, except the sherry, and cover with a cartouche of baking paper. Bring to the boil, then turn down to a slow simmer and cook for about 30 minutes, before checking—just inside the leg—that the bird is just cooked. Next, turn off the heat and leave it in the water for 10 minutes, then remove the bird and cover it with foil.

> Bring the poaching liquor back to the boil, reduce until it's flavoursome, then strain or pass it through a sieve. In a clean pan, add the sherry and reduce until syrupy, then add the strained poaching liquor and reduce to about 600ml.

> Next, make a thick roux by melting the butter in a pan, adding the sieved flour and mixing to a paste.

> Cook the roux for several minutes, then gradually start adding the pheasant stock, stirring all the time, until it becomes a thick

sauce. Add the chopped herbs and cream, then check for seasoning.

> Remove the breasts from the pheasant, shred them by pulling the meat lengthways between two forks, add to the sauce and keep warm.

> Finally, to make the crumble topping, melt the butter in a frying pan, add the breadcrumbs and stir constantly until they are golden and crispy. Turn them on to

kitchen paper to soak up the excess butter and add the Parmesan cheese. Next, cook the bacon rashers until they are crispy enough to crumble into medium fine pieces and add them to the breadcrumbs.

> Place the pheasant and sauce mixture into a pie dish, sprinkle with the crumble and finish in the oven at 180°C/350°F/gas mark 4 until heated through.

> '**I got this recipe from someone I know. It is delicious. I invented a grouse one, too, Coq au Vin with Grouse, as well as Moussaka with Grouse (it doesn't always have to be lamb), in other words Groussaka!**'

King Charles III

to be very well hung", but hanging should only be taking place for 4–6 days, really, before the feathers have been removed and it's been gutted; just enough to make sure it's tender and ready for the table.' Thoughtful preparation is equally as important. 'When I'm cooking grouse, I always clean away the bit by the stomach—it's slightly acrid and I don't think people want to eat that. You simply have to go about these things the right way.'

Mr Williams's culinary love affair with all things furred and feathered survived his move to the capital in 1975, after which he worked at the Royal Garden Hotel in Kensington, The Berkeley and Claridge's, before arriving at The Ritz in 2004 (he was made an MBE for services to the hospitality industry in 2008).

He's passionate about provenance and has worked with the same suppliers for decades. 'Most of what we serve here is delivered by a chap I've known since he was 18 years old and who has great relationships with the guys up in North Yorkshire. He knows exactly what I'm looking for: good hanging and, when the birds

are cleaned, for them to have been cleaned dry. A wet pluck is the worst thing in the world—washing the bird washes away flavour.'

His face lights up when he describes the dish His Majesty calls his favourite: pheasant crumble pie. 'We poach the pheasant very gently on the bone, so that it retains its moisture,' he explains. 'Then, we break it down with the stock, make a reduction, thicken that a touch to create a sauce, add a bit of cream and pour it over the bird. After that, we simply top it with the crumble and bake it in the oven. That's it! It's very wholesome and very enjoyable to eat.'

He and his 65-strong brigade at The Ritz have made an art form of game cookery, yet he insists you don't have to be a professional to create something really impressive. 'The most important thing is not to overcook game birds,' he says. 'Cook them to the point you enjoy, but make sure there's juice inside. If you're starting out, I'd recommend doing a roast: pheasant, partridge, perhaps wild duck. Just check you're using enough fat, as game birds are very lean.'

Mr Williams adds: 'For me, 180˚C is the magic oven temperature and they don't take long—a grouse, say, can be cooked in as little as 10 minutes. Make sure you baste yours really well, then let it rest for a good 15 or 20 minutes at a nice, ambient temperature.'

At a time when you can walk into a supermarket and leave with the same basket of shopping in January and July, the chef is sceptical about our demand for year-round availability of food. 'Seasonality, of the kind you get with game, brings something new to the table,' he says. 'We work on the principle that the ingredients the animals live among tend to go really well with them, so we serve our dish of roast grouse with blackberries and ceps. It's very simple.'

Mr Williams beams. 'I think that's the best way to eat.' ♔

For recipes from the hotel, see John Williams's 'The Ritz London: The Cookbook' (020–7493 8181; www.theritzlondon.com/cookbook). Giandomenico Scanu, the hotel's tea master, has created a special blend of loose-leaf tea to honour the coronation

Coronation quiche

Buckingham Palace calls this as 'deep quiche with a crisp, light pastry case and delicate flavours of spinach, broad beans and fresh tarragon. Eat hot or cold with a green salad and boiled new potatoes'

YOU'LL NEED 1x 20cm (8in) flan tin
SERVES 6

INGREDIENTS

Pastry	Filling
125g plain flour	125ml milk
Pinch of salt	175ml double cream
25g cold butter, diced	2 medium eggs
25g lard	1tbspn chopped fresh tarragon
2tbspn milk	Salt and pepper
	100g grated cheddar cheese
OR 1x 250g block of ready-made shortcrust pastry	180g cooked spinach, lightly chopped
	60g cooked broad beans or soya beans

METHOD

To make the pastry

> Sieve the flour and salt into a bowl; add the fats and rub the mixture together using your finger tips until you get a sandy, breadcrumb like texture.

> Add the milk a little at a time and bring the ingredients together into a dough.

> Cover and allow to rest in the fridge for 30–45 minutes.

> Lightly flour the work surface and roll out the pastry to a circle a little larger than the top of the tin and about 5mm thick.

> Line the tin with the pastry, taking care not to have any holes or the mixture could leak. Cover and rest for a further 30 minutes in the fridge.

> Preheat the oven to 190°C/375°F/gas mark 5.

> Line the pastry case with greaseproof paper, add baking beans and bake blind for 15 minutes, before removing the greaseproof paper and baking beans.

> Reduce the oven temperature to 160°C/325°/gas mark 3.

> Beat together the milk, cream, eggs, herbs and seasoning.

> Scatter half of the grated cheese in the blind-baked base, top with the chopped spinach and beans and herbs, then pour over the liquid mixture.

> If required, gently give the mixture a delicate stir to ensure the filling is evenly dispersed, but be careful not to damage the pastry case.

> Sprinkle over the remaining cheese. Place into the oven and bake for 20–25 minutes until set and lightly golden.

Coin of the realm

Sculptor Martin Jennings created the likeness that will adorn The King's coins. He tells **Timothy Mowl** about portraying character in his work and how he approached the commission from the Royal Mint

Photographs by Mark Williamson

Far left: **Martin Jennings gathers his tools in his Gloucestershire studio.** *Above:* **A disc bearing the bas-relief image of The King**

TRAVELLERS hurrying for trains across the upper concourse of St Pancras Station in London cannot fail to catch sight of the bronze statue of Sir John Betjeman. It is an intensely humane, sensitive portrait of the nation's favourite poet. He wears a shabby overcoat, his waistcoat bulges a little due to an incipient paunch and he carries a shopping bag. With a hand on his crumpled trilby, he looks up to the cast-iron Victorian roof, which, as an ardent conservationist, he had campaigned to save from demolition. It is as if he has just taken a breath in wonderment at the beauty of it all.

This conscious lifting into the air of the weight of a sculpture is a particular artistic signature of Martin Jennings, who fashioned the statue. It gives a seemingly inert artwork that dynamic sense of animation, of movement. At Broadcasting House, Mr Jennings's George Orwell wags his roll-up cigarette at passer-bys from his plinth-soapbox—'Big Brother is Watching You!'—and his Philip Larkin, gabardine mac flapping, dashes from Hull's Paragon Station to make his Whitsun train journey to King's Cross. In his most striking sculpture to date, the Jamaican nurse Mary Seacole strides out at St Thomas's Hospital, in the sculptor's words, 'marching defiantly onward into an oncoming wind, as if confronting head on some of the personal resistance she had constantly to battle'.

We met at his favourite café by his workshop, which is housed in a former schoolhouse at Chalford, near Stroud in Gloucestershire. The move to this semi-industrial Cotswold valley has been felicitous, in that Mr Jennings now has huge spaces to accommodate big →

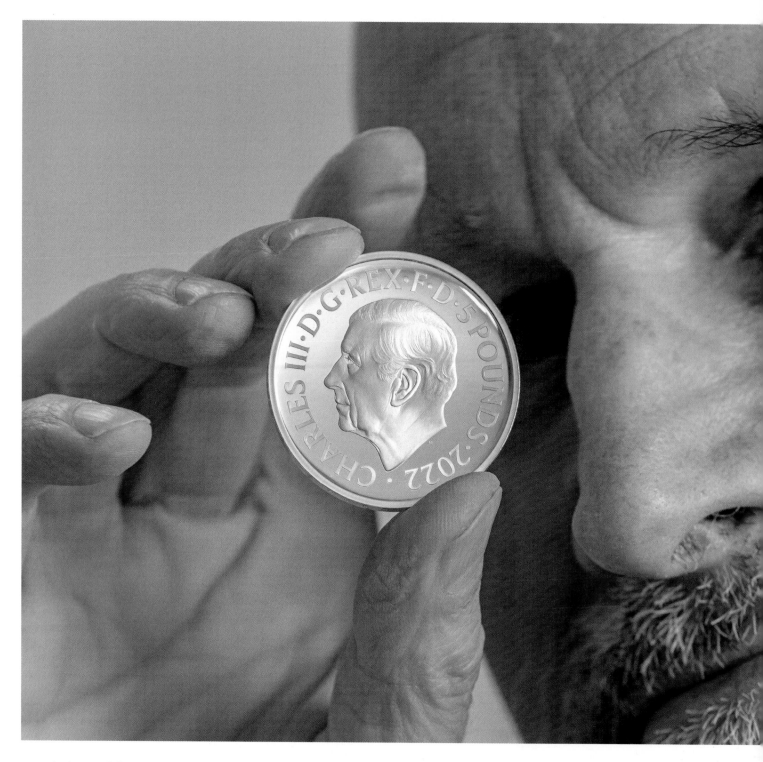

commissions and the studio is next door to the Pangolin Editions foundry that casts his sculptures. Over hearty soup and toasted sandwiches, Mr Jennings conveyed his passion for sculpture: 'I love it when something breaks out of its early structural stage and begins to take on a life of its own.' A vital part of this process is concentrated research. 'You have to embed yourself in the life of your subject and choose a pose that best expresses their essential self'.

One new commission is for a bronze of John Keats to be sited in Moorgate, London EC2, close to the poet's birthplace. For this, Mr Jennings has decided against an idealised realisation and has taken instead the poet's life mask for his model. The finished sculpture will be twice life size and set on a slender plinth. He has been reading the poet's *Odes* to get a feel of the man and to choose an appropriate inscription; most of his sculptures are enhanced with quotations from their subjects' works. The lines from his *Ode on Indolence* will convey Keats's tenet that poetry is founded in a state of being halfway between wakefulness and sleep.

Mr Jennings is, without question, the most gifted figurative sculptor of his generation. He came to sculpture in the 1980s after attending a course at the Sir John Cass School of Art in Whitechapel. Commissioned by many national institutions, including the National

A coin for a Carolean reign: the profile pose faces left in contrast with the late Queen

Portrait Gallery, St Paul's Cathedral, the Palace of Westminster, the University of Oxford and the National Memorial Arboretum, he won the Public Monuments and Sculpture Association Marsh Award for his *Women of Steel* sculpture in Sheffield and for his *George Orwell* at the BBC, a bust taken from which is in the library at Eton College in Berkshire.

His latest artistic endeavour is in an entirely different field, that of numismatics, having been asked last year to design the effigy for Charles III's new coinage. Kevin Clancy, secretary of the Royal Mint Advisory

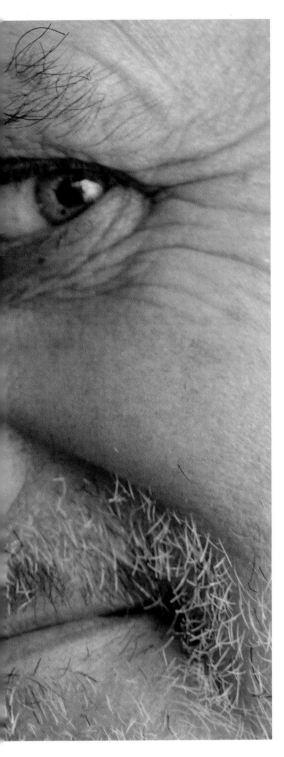

by an inscription. Successive monarchs have traditionally alternated left-right, apart from Edward VIII, who wanted to show his best side on the coinage. Mr Jennings made preliminary drawings for a bas-relief sculpture, which was then modelled in 'plastilene', a soft, oil-based compound, which we know from our school days as plasticine, on an MDF disc, to produce a cream-coloured relief of the effigy. The size of the model is that of a large dinner plate, or as Mr Jennings puts it, 'an out-stretched hand that, when reduced for the coinage, becomes the size of a fingernail'.

> ‘ He feels awed to know the coin "will be seen and held by people around the world for centuries" ’

The Royal Mint has moved from a complex analogue process for producing coins, which involved rubber moulds that were plated with nickel and backed up with copper, to a fully digitised system in which the artwork is photographed and three-dimensional computer packages are used to manipulate the image and align it with the surrounding inscription. The cutting machine is powered by lasers to produce a negative die, from which the coins are minted. Mr Jennings was particularly concerned that the effigy should integrate seamlessly with the inscription. He worked with the Royal Mint's in-house designers to lay out inscriptions for all the denominations, using a robust font and ensuring stylistic coherence throughout—

the sculptor stresses that the entire venture has been one of artistic collaboration with the Mint's design team and its 'remarkable fabrication process'.

Mr Jennings crafted the effigy from photographs and it was then sent to The King for his approval after the death of the Queen. Dr Clancy reports that the monarch made suggestions for minor changes, but was very happy with the image. Indeed, the design has been used for the new stamps of the realm.

There is a further link between Mr Jennings, Betjeman and the national coinage. The poet was a member of the Mint's Advisory Committee on the Design of Coins, Medals, Seals and Decorations. This is a Government body of advisers, which was chaired by the late Duke of Edinburgh during Betjeman's tenure. When Arnold Machin was chosen in 1964 to design the new decimalisation coinage, which was eventually introduced in 1968, Betjeman, in a typically arch aside, told Machin that his effigy of Elizabeth II 'made her look a bit sexy'. This humanising of the symbol of monarchy is something Humphrey Paget achieved with his effigy for Edward VIII, coins of which were never in general circulation, and his relief design for George VI. Mr Jennings had Paget's effigies very much in mind when he designed his relief for Charles III, aiming to give warmth to the portrait, making The King more human and accessible. Taking Paget as his inspiration also seemed appropriate in that his effigy of Charles III relates back to The King's grandfather and, as such, displays distinct family likeness.

The coin effigy is the smallest work of art that Mr Jennings has created and he feels awed to know 'that it will be seen and held by people around the world for centuries to come'. ♛

Committee and director of the Royal Mint Museum, remarks that it is 'an amazing achievement to create such an accomplished portrait from a standing start'. Unlike most medal and coin designers, Mr Jennings had little experience of the art form, but he had previously entered a Royal Mint competition and was known to the director through Dr Clancy's support of the Society of Portrait Sculptors, of which Mr Jennings is a member. He had, therefore, been in the Royal Mint's sights for some time and was a natural choice when it became clear that the Prince of Wales would soon ascend to the throne.

The commission was for a bare-headed portrait effigy of The King facing left, encircled

Revelling in royalty

Street parties and celebrations
from across the land

Enthusiasts lined the Mall for days ahead of the big day, hoping to catch a glimpse of The King and Queen, and made sure that they were dressed for the occasion

A knitted tribute to The Prince and Princess of Wales in Windsor

Left: An amusingly decorated telephone box in the Surrey village of Compton. *Right:* The Elizabeth Line didn't forget to celebrate

Dancing in the rain: children play in puddles at Cardiff Castle, where the ceremony was broadcast on screens for the assembled crowds

US citizen Donna Werner is no stranger to royal celebrations, having travelled to the UK for three decades to celebrate occasions

Does my head look big in this? Onlookers sport their paper crowns

Left: **A fabulous floral tribute adorns the front door of a home in Windsor, Berkshire.** *Right:* **One reveller makes his feelings known**

Left: **Prime Minister Rishi Sunak spreads the joy at the Downing Street Lunch Party.** *Right:* **A little girl can't hide her excitement**

Left: **Three cheers! A street party in St Cuthbert's Road in London.**
Above: **A young lady watches the procession from her window**

Left: **A crowd gathers near Trafalgar Square awaiting the new King.** *Right:* **Dressed to impress: a resident of Alfriston, East Sussex**

Get up and dance

A celebratory concert brings the
coronation weekend to a crescendo

Francesca Hayward and Marcelino Sambé, principal dancers with the Royal Ballet, perform a piece of bespoke choreography for Their Majesties

Nigerian superstar Tiwa Savage performed *Keys to the Kingdom*, a reference to the words of wisdom offered by Mufasa to his son Simba in *The Lion King*

The King, Queen and Royal Family were joined by notable names, such as Sir Keir Starmer, Rishi Sunak, Baroness Scotland and, for a brief cameo, Muppets star Kermit the frog

Above: Hector Bajcer holds a flag in the crowd, complete with bearskin. *Right:* Lucy Illingworth dazzles on the piano

Getty; Alamy

Paloma Faith performed hits such as the energetic *Lullaby* in a voluminous fuchsia gown by Roksanda

Left: Lionel Richie's *All Night Long* even had The King dancing. *Above:* The Prince of Wales gives a touching address to the crowd and his father

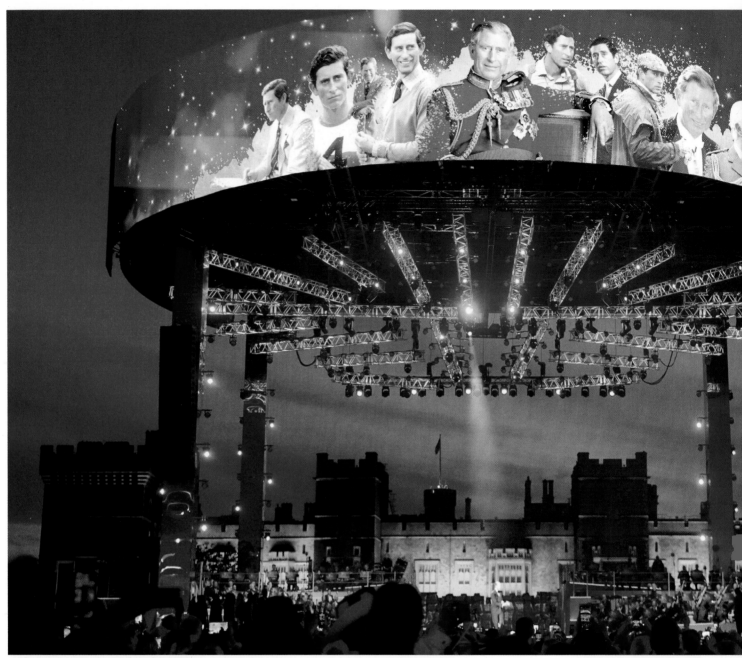

Left: **For the first time in three years, Take That took to the stage to perform several of their hits.** *Right:* **Fresh from singing the Kyrie Eleison in the coronation ceremony, Welsh bass-baritone Bryn Terfel was joined on stage by the legendary blind Italian tenor Andrea Bocelli**

The enormous stage was situated on the East Lawn against the backdrop of Windsor Castle

Above: **Close to The King's heart: as well as dazzling the crowds, US singer Katy Perry is an ambassador for his anti-child-trafficking charity British Asian Trust.** *Below:* **New *Doctor Who* Ncuti Gatwa and *My Neighbour Totoro* star Mei Mac join forces to perform Act I, Scene V of Shakespeare's *Romeo & Juliet*, supported by the Royal Shakespeare Company, the Royal College of Art, the Royal College of Music, the Royal Opera House and the Royal Ballet** ♔

The final countdown

From one (crown) to 300 million (people),
the coronation is a numbers game, finds **Agnes Stamp**

300 million

About **300** million worldwide tuned in to watch the coronation on television

TWO

TWO of The King's horses raced after the Coronation Service. The royal colours were borne by Candle Of Hope in the Conqueror Fillies' Stakes (1.55pm at Goodwood) and Saga in the Howden Suffolk Stakes (3.25pm at Newmarket); Saga came second

4000

4,000 members of the British Armed Forces escorted the Coronation Procession back to Buckingham Palace

FIRST

The King is the **FIRST** reigning monarch to hold a university degree (he read History at Trinity College, Cambridge)

More than 400

More than **400** personnel, across **13** locations and deployed Royal Navy ships, fired **21** rounds to mark the coronation, with the exception of the Tower of London and Horse Guards Parade, where a **62**-round salute and a **six**-gun salvo were fired respectively

TWELVE

12 newly commissioned works—consisting of **SIX** orchestral commissions, **FIVE** choral commissions and **ONE** organ commission—were performed at the service, showcasing musical talent from across the UK and the Commonwealth

Four

Prince Charles was **FOUR** years old when he attended his mother's coronation in 1953. The King's children were **40** and **38** years old when they attended their father's

COUNTRY LIFE has reported on **FOUR** coronations to date. The coronation of Charles III is our **FIFTH**

2200

The final guest list made up a congregation of more than **2,200** people and included members of the Royal Family, representatives from **203** countries and about **100** heads of state

The Sceptre with Cross features the **530.2-carat** Cullinan I—or the Star of Africa—diamond

ONE

ONE grey police horse, Wilbur, acted as 'pointer' and led the King's and Coronation Procession to and from Westminster Abbey

FIRST

William III and Mary II were the **FIRST** (and only) couple crowned joint monarchs of England, in April 1689

1.3 miles

The King and Queen Consort took the same **1.3**-mile route from Buckingham Palace to the ceremony at Westminster Abbey and back again

120

More than **120** varieties of flowers were grown for the Coronation Service by more than **80** members of Flowers from the Farm across the **FOUR** nations of the UK

£3bn to £5bn

The Crown Jewels have been estimated to be worth anywhere between **£3 billion** to **£5 billion**

£5, £10, £20 & £50

FOUR new banknote designs (£5, £10, £20 and £50) featuring Charles III were revealed on **December 20, 2022**. The new notes won't be in circulation until **2024**

4lb 12oz

The solid gold frame of **St Edward's Crown** (which is used at the moment of crowning itself) weighs **4lb 12oz**

7000

7,000 ceremonial troops lined the streets of central London, standing to attention in **FIVE**-pace intervals

SIX

The Coronation Service fell into **SIX** parts: the Recognition, the Oath, the Anointing, the Investiture (which includes the crowning), the Enthronement and the Homage

447

447 additional armed-forces personnel from **56** nations and realms were on parade to mark the historic moment

73

The King, at the age of **73**, became the oldest person to accede to the British throne last September. The previous record holder was William IV, who was **64** when he became King in **1830**

This will be the **THIRD** coronation broadcast by the BBC

Two minutes and thirty seconds

The **TWO** MINUTES AND **30** SECONDS flypast over the Mall featured **nine** helicopters and **nine** Hawk fast jets from the Royal Air Force aerobatic team the Red Arrows. Bad weather curtailed the original plan for a **SIX** MINUTE flypast, which would have included **68** aircraft (including **16** helicopters) from all **THREE** services (the Royal Navy, British Army and Royal Air Force)

Three

cheers for The King—hip, hip, hooray! ♕

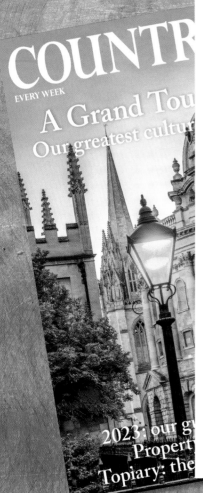

50
NOVELTY CAKES
& PARTY CAKES

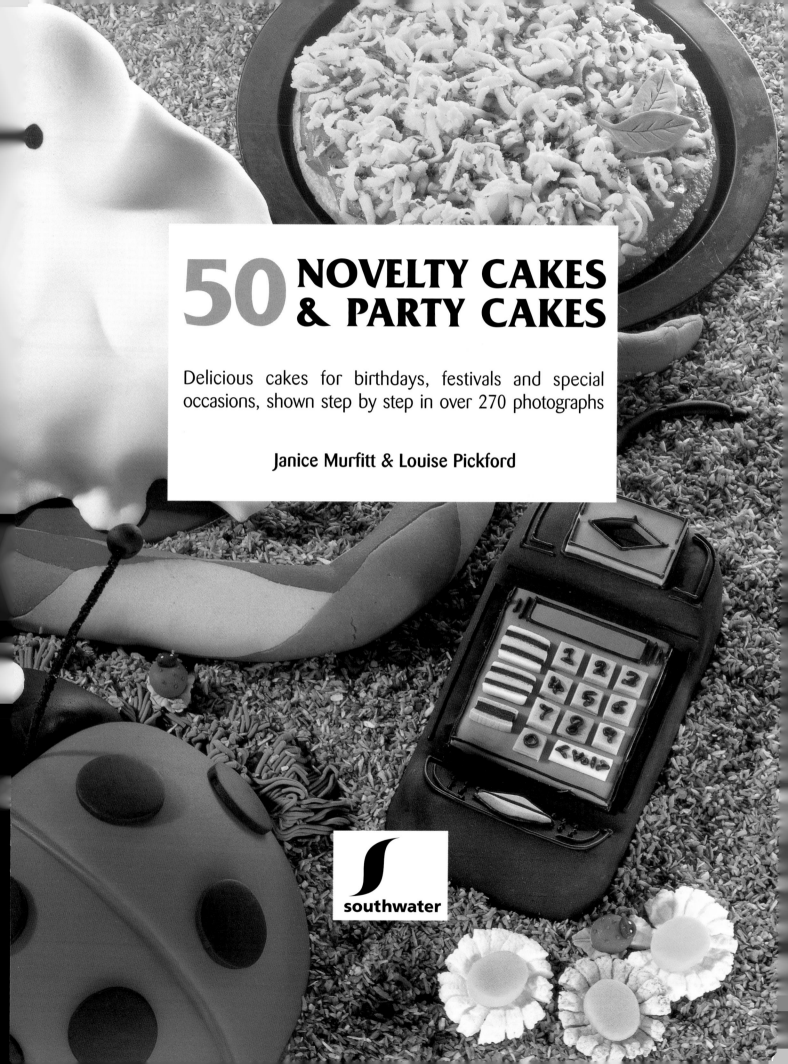

This edition is published by Southwater, an imprint of Anness Publishing Ltd
Hermes House, 88–89 Blackfriars Road, London SE1 8HA; tel. 020 7401 2077; fax 020 7633 9499

www.southwaterbooks.com; www.annesspublishing.com

If you like the images in this book and would like to investigate using them for publishing, promotions or
advertising, please visit our website www.practicalpictures.com for more information.

UK agent: The Manning Partnership Ltd; tel. 01225 478444; fax 01225 478440; sales@manning-partnership.co.uk
UK distributor: Grantham Book Services Ltd; tel. 01476 541080; fax 01476 541061; orders@gbs.tbs-ltd.co.uk
North American agent/distributor: National Book Network; tel. 301 459 3366; fax 301 429 5746;
www.nbnbooks.com
Australian agent/distributor: Pan Macmillan Australia; tel. 1300 135 113; fax 1300 135 103;
customer.service@macmillan.com.au
New Zealand agent/distributor: David Bateman Ltd; tel. (09) 415 7664; fax (09) 415 8892

ETHICAL TRADING POLICY
Because of our ongoing ecological investment programme, you, as our customer, can have the
pleasure and reassurance of knowing that a tree is being cultivated on your behalf to naturally
replace the materials used to make the book you are holding. For further information about this
scheme, go to www.annesspublishing.com/trees

Publisher: Joanna Lorenz
Project Editor: Judith Simons
Art Director: Peter Bridgewater
Designer: James Lawrence
Photographer: David Armstrong
Contributors: Janice Murfitt, Angela Nilsen, Sarah Maxwell, Joanna Farrow, Louise Pickford

© Anness Publishing Ltd 1993, 2007

Previously published as *Party Cakes*

MEASUREMENTS
Three sets of measurements have been provided in the recipes here, with quantities given in both metric and
imperial measures and, where appropriate, in standard cups and spoons. Follow one set, but not a mixture, because
they are not interchangeable.
Standard spoon and cup measures are level. 1 tsp = 5ml, 1 tbsp = 15ml, 1 cup = 250ml/8fl oz
Australian standard tablespoons are 20ml. Australian readers should use 3 tsp in place of 1 tbsp for measuring small
quantities of gelatine, flour, salt etc.
American pints are 16fl oz/2 cups. American readers should use 20fl oz/2.5 cups in place of 1 pint when
measuring liquids.
Electric oven temperatures in this book are for conventional ovens. When using a fan oven, the temperature will
probably need to be reduced by about 10–20°C/20–40°F. Since ovens vary, you should check with your
manufacturer's instruction book for guidance.
Medium (US large) eggs are used unless otherwise stated.

CONTENTS

A NOVELTY CAKE is a wonderful way to celebrate a special event or birthday, and can provide an amusing twist to traditional occasions. In the following pages, there are original cake designs for recipients of all ages, as well as unusual cakes for anniversaries and seasonal celebrations. For the kids, for instance, there are birthday balloons, a merry-go-round, or a jolly coloured snake; for adults there are cakes to suit every special interest – a mobile phone, a sailing boat, even a terracotta flower pot. There is a sophisticated egg timbale for an Easter table, and a beautiful hand-painted festive cake for Christmas.

The cakes are all highly distinctive but not too difficult to achieve. There are creations using coloured sugarpaste or fondant, royal icing, butter icing, various frostings and flavoured icings. A whole range of special decorating techniques are described and explained step by step, so you can build up a whole repertoire of cake effects. A basket of strawberries is created from basketweave piping with chocolate butter icing; a candle cake shows how to marble coloured sugarpaste; a present-shaped cake uses inlaid sugarpaste in contrasting colours to spectacular effect. Follow the projects exactly or adapt the techniques to suit your own occasions.

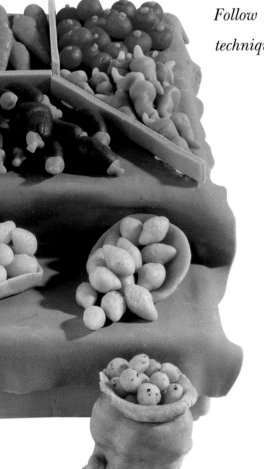

A BASKET OF STRAWBERRIES

Quick and easy to make, a perfect surprise for a birthday or Valentine's day. And don't be put off by the icing technique – it's much easier than it looks!

INGREDIENTS

Serves 6–8
- 2-egg quantity quick-mix sponge cake
- 45 ml/3 tbsp/3 tbsp apricot glaze
- 675 g/1½ lb/1½ lb commercial or homemade marzipan
- icing (confectioners') sugar, for dusting
- 50 g/2 oz/4 tbsp caster (superfine) sugar
- 350 g/12 oz/¾ lb chocolate-flavoured butter icing
- red food colouring

MATERIALS AND EQUIPMENT

- 450 g/1 lb/3 cup loaf tin (bread pan)
- 18 cm/7 in oval cakeboard
- piping bag fitted with a small star nozzle
- 10 plastic strawberry stalks
- 30 × 7.5 cm/12 × 3 in strip kitchen foil
- 30 cm/12 in thin red ribbon

STORING

The cake can be made up to two days in advance, wrapped in foil and stored in an airtight container. The finished cake can be refrigerated for up to one week.

FREEZING

The un-iced cake can be frozen for up to three months.

VARIATION

For a Get Well cake, fill the basket with a selection of different shaped marzipan fruits. For a keen gardener, fill with marzipan vegetables.

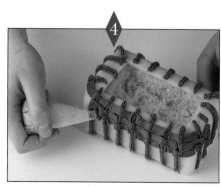

1 Preheat the oven to 180°C/350°F/Gas 4. Grease and line the base and sides of a 450 g/1 lb/3 cup loaf tin (bread pan). Spoon the cake mixture into the prepared tin (pan) and smooth the top with a plastic spatula. Bake in the preheated oven for 40–50 minutes, or until a skewer inserted into the middle of the cake comes out clean. Leave for 5 minutes before turning out on to a wire rack to cool.

2 Slice a thin layer off the top of the cake to make it perfectly flat. Score a 5 mm/¼ in border around the edge of the cake and scrape out the insides to make a shallow hollow.

3 Place the cake in the middle of the cakeboard and brush the sides and border edges with the apricot glaze. Roll out 275 g/10 oz/10 oz of the marzipan on a surface lightly dusted with icing (confectioners') sugar. Cut the marzipan into rectangles and use to cover the sides of the cake, overlapping the border edges. Gently press the edges of the marzipan together to seal.

4 Fill the piping bag with the butter icing. Pipe vertical lines about 2.5 cm/1 in apart all around the sides of the cake. Starting at the top of the cake pipe short horizontal lines alternately crossing over and then stopping at the vertical lines to give a basket-weave effect. Pipe a decorative line of icing around the top edge of the basket, to finish.

5 Colour the remaining marzipan with the red food colouring and mould into strawberry shapes. Roll in caster (superfine) sugar and press a plastic stalk into the top of each one. Carefully arrange the strawberries in the basket.

6 *To make the basket handle, fold the foil into a thin strip and wind the ribbon evenly around it to cover completely. Bend into a curve and push the ends into the sides of the cake. Decorate with ribbon bows.*

MERMAID

This mermaid cake would make a splash at any little girl's birthday party! The scales can be cut out using a 2.5 cm/1 in plain round cutter, then cut in half, if you don't have a crescent-shaped one. Use seashells, starfish or any other sea objects of your choice to decorate the sand.

INGREDIENTS

Serves 6–8

- *2-egg quantity quick-mix sponge cake*
- *175 g/6 oz/6 oz butter icing*
- *25 g/1 oz/1 oz plain popcorn*
- *450 g/1 lb/1 lb milk chocolate, melted*
- *icing (confectioners') sugar, for dusting*
- *225 g/8 oz/½ lb homemade or commercial marzipan*
- *225 g/8 oz/½ lb sugarpaste (fondant) icing*
- *pink food colouring*
- *1 egg white, lightly beaten*
- *a little sunflower oil*
- *75 g/3 oz/6 tbsp demerara sugar (granulated brown sugar) for the sand*

MATERIALS AND EQUIPMENT

- *1.1 l/2 pt/5 cup pudding basin (bowl)*
- *25 cm/10 in fluted cakeboard*
- *1 × doll, similar in dimensions to a 'Barbie' or 'Sindy' doll*
- *1 small crescent-shaped cutter*
- *small scallop shell or shell-shaped chocolate mould*

STORING

The cake can be made up to two days in advance, wrapped in foil and stored in an airtight container. The finished cake can be stored for three to four days in a cool, dry place.

FREEZING

The un-iced cake can be frozen for up to three months.

VARIATION

Flavour the sponge cake and butter icing with chocolate to make this an ideal choice for chocoholic children.

1 *Preheat the oven to 180°C/350°F/Gas 4. Grease and base-line a 1.1 l/2 pint/ 5 cup pudding basin (bowl). Spoon the cake mixture into the prepared basin (bowl) and smooth the surface with a plastic spatula. Bake in the preheated oven for 40–50 minutes, or until a skewer inserted into the middle of the cake comes out clean. Leave for 5 minutes before turning out onto a wire rack to cool.*

2 *Place the cake flat side down on the work surface and cut across into 3 layers of equal thickness. Spread the bottom layer with two-thirds of the butter icing. Place the second layer of sponge cake on top and spread with the remaining butter icing. Top with the remaining piece of sponge cake. Position slightly off-centre on the cakeboard and set aside.*

3 *Mix the popcorn with about one-third of the melted chocolate and spoon around the base and up the sides of the cake. Pour the remaining melted chocolate over the top of the cake to cover completely. Leave to set at room temperature.*

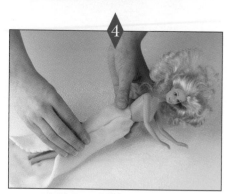

4 *Lightly dust the work surface with icing (confectioners') sugar and roll out half of the marzipan to an oblong shape, wide enough to wrap around the doll's legs and 5 cm/2 in longer. Use to surround her legs, starting at the waist and working down-wards. Mould the bottom section into a fin-shaped tail. Position the doll so she is sitting on the cake.*

5 *Divide the sugarpaste (fondant) in half; colour one half dark pink and the other half light pink with pink food colouring. Thinly roll out the dark pink sugarpaste (fondant) on a work surface lightly dusted with icing (confectioners') sugar. Reserve a small piece of the sugarpaste (fondant) to make the mermaid's top. Cut out 'scales' with a small crescent-shaped cutter, keeping the cut scales covered with a sheet of cling film (plastic wrap) to stop them drying out. Thinly roll out the light pink sugarpaste (fondant) icing and continue to cut out the scales in the same way.*

6 *To make the bodice, press the reserved piece of dark pink sugarpaste (fondant) icing over an oiled tiny scallop shell, or into an oiled shell-shaped chocolate mould. Gently remove the sugarpaste (fondant) from the mould and trim the edges. Brush with a little egg white and stick in place for the mermaid's top.*

Brush each scale with a little egg white and, starting at the fin end, stick on to the tail in overlapping rows, until the marzipan is completely covered.

6

7 *Sprinkle the cakeboard with demerara (granulated brown) sugar for the sand and decorate with seashells, starfish or any other sea objects of your choice.*

LADYBIRD

Create a little animal magic and make this cake for a nature lover or gardener.

INGREDIENTS

Serves 10–12

- 3-egg quantity lemon-flavoured quick mix sponge cake
- 175 g/6 oz/6 oz lemon-flavoured butter icing
- 60 ml/4 tbsp/4 tbsp lemon curd, warmed
- icing (confectioners') sugar, for dusting
- good 1 kg/2 lb 6 oz/2 lb 6 oz sugarpaste (fondant) icing
- red, black and green food colourings
- 5 marshmallows
- 50 g/2 oz/2 oz golden commercial or homemade marzipan
- edible ladybird (ladybug) icing decorations (optional)

MATERIALS AND EQUIPMENT

- 1.1 l/2 pt/5 cup ovenproof mixing bowl
- greaseproof (wax) paper
- wooden skewer
- 28 cm/11 in round cakeboard
- 4 cm/1½ in plain round biscuit (cookie) cutter
- 5 cm/2 in plain round biscuit (cookie) cutter
- garlic press
- 2 pipe cleaners

STORING

The cake can be made up to two days in advance, wrapped in foil and stored in an airtight container. The finished cake, covered in sugarpaste (fondant), can be stored for three to four days in a cool, dry place.

FREEZING

The un-iced cake can be frozen for up to three months.

VARIATION

Marzipan works just as well as a covering for this cake.

1 Preheat the oven to 180°C/350°F/Gas 4. Grease and line the base of a 1.1 l/2 pt/5 cup ovenproof mixing bowl. Spoon the mixture into the prepared bowl and smooth the surface with a plastic spatula. Bake in the preheated oven for 55–60 minutes, or until a skewer inserted into the centre of the cake comes out clean. Leave for 5 minutes before turning out on to a wire rack to cool.

2 Cut the cake across in half and sandwich together with the butter icing. Cut vertically through the cake, about a third of the way in. Brush both pieces of cake with the lemon curd.

3 Colour 450 g/1 lb/1 lb sugarpaste (fondant) icing red, with red food colouring. Lightly dust the work surface with icing (confectioners') sugar and roll out the red sugarpaste (fondant) to about 5 mm/¼ in thick. Use to cover the larger piece of cake to make the ladybird's body. Use a wooden skewer or the back of a knife to make an indentation down the centre of the cake for the wings.

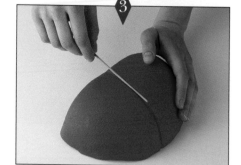

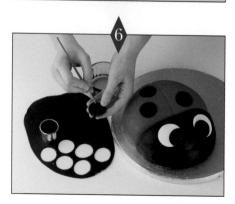

4 Colour 350 g/12 oz/¾ lb sugarpaste (fondant) icing black, with black food colouring. Roll out three-quarters of the black sugarpaste (fondant) and use to cover the smaller piece of cake for the ladybird's head. Place the cakes on the cakeboard, assembling the ladybird and lightly pressing the head and body together to shape.

5 Roll out 50 g/2 oz/2 oz sugarpaste (fondant) icing and cut out two circles with a 5 cm/2 in round biscuit (cookie) cutter for the eyes. Brush with a little water and stick in position on the head.

6 Roll out the remaining black sugarpaste (fondant) icing thinly. Use to cut out eight circles with a 4 cm/1½ in round biscuit (cookie) cutter. Use two of these rounds for the eyes and stick the others on to the body with a little water. Reserve the trimmings.

7 Colour 225 g/8 oz/½ lb sugarpaste (fondant) icing green. To make the grass, break off pieces of green sugarpaste (fondant) and squeeze through a garlic press. Trim off with a knife. Brush the board around the ladybird with a little water and gently stick down the grass.

8 *To make the marshmallow flowers, roll the marzipan into a 2 cm/¾ in long sausage shape and cut into slices to make rounds. Set aside. Dust the work surface with a little icing (confectioners') sugar and flatten each marshmallow with a rolling pin, sprinkling with more icing (confectioners') sugar to prevent sticking. Using scissors, snip from the outside edge towards the middle of each marshmallow to make the petals. Press a marzipan round into the middle of each flower and use to decorate the cake.*

9 *To make the antennae, paint the pipe cleaners with black food colouring and press a small ball of the remaining black sugarpaste (fondant) on to the end of each one. Bend each pipe cleaner slightly and insert it into the cake between the head and the body. Arrange the decorations around the cake, if using.*

PIZZA CAKE

Quick, easy and impressive – a definite winner
for pizza fanatics everywhere.

INGREDIENTS

Serves 8–10
- 2-egg quantity quick-mix
  sponge cake
- 350 g/12 oz/³⁄₄ lb butter icing,
  coloured red
- 175 g/6 oz/6 oz yellow commercial
  or homemade marzipan
- 15 ml/1 tbsp/1 tbsp desiccated
  (dry unsweetened shredded) coconut
- red and green food colouring
- icing (confectioners') sugar,
  for dredging
- 25 g/1 oz/1 oz sugarpaste
  (fondant) icing

MATERIALS AND EQUIPMENT

- 23 cm/9 in shallow cake tin (pan)
- greaseproof (wax) paper
- 25 cm/10 in pizza plate
- cheese grater
- a leaf cutter or stencil

STORING

The cake can be made up to two
days in advance, wrapped in foil and
stored in an airtight container. The
finished cake can be refrigerated for
up to one week.

FREEZING

The un-iced cake can be frozen for
up to three months.

1 Preheat the oven to 180°C/350°F/Gas 4.
Grease and line the base of a 23 cm/9 in
shallow cake tin (pan). Spoon the mixture
into the prepared tin (pan) and smooth the
surface with a plastic spatula. Bake in the
preheated oven for 40–50 minutes, or until
a skewer inserted into the centre of the cake
comes out clean. Leave for 5 minutes before
turning out onto a wire rack to cool.

2 Place the cake on the pizza plate and
spread evenly with the red butter icing,
leaving a 1 cm/½ in border around the edge.

3 Knead the marzipan for a few minutes,
to soften slightly, then grate it in the
same way as grating cheese. Use to sprinkle
over the red butter icing.

4 Colour the sugarpaste (fondant) icing
green with green food colouring. For the
leaf garnish, lightly dust the work surface
with icing (confectioners') sugar and roll out
the green sugarpaste (fondant) to about 5 mm/
¼ in thick. Use the leaf cutter or stencil to
cut out two leaf shapes. Garnish the pizza
cake with the sugarpaste (fondant) leaves.

5 To make the chopped herbs, place the
desiccated (dry unsweetened shredded)
coconut in a small bowl and add enough
green food colouring to make it dark green,
stirring after each addition of colouring.

6 Scatter the coconut herbs over the
pizza cake.

THE BEAUTIFUL
PRESENT CAKE

For a best friend, mother, aunt, grandmother or sister, this beautiful cake is fitting for any occasion.

INGREDIENTS

Serves 15–20

- 4-egg quantity vanilla-flavoured quick-mix sponge cake
- 350 g/12 oz/³/₄ lb vanilla-flavoured butter icing
- 60 ml/4 tbsp/4 tbsp apricot glaze
- icing (confectioners') sugar, for dusting
- 575 g/1¼ lb/1¼ lb homemade or commercial marzipan
- 850 g/1 lb 14 oz/1 lb 14 oz sugarpaste (fondant) icing
- purple and pink food colouring
- cold water, for brushing

MATERIALS AND EQUIPMENT

- 23 cm/9 in square cake tin (pan)
- 25 cm/10 in square cakeboard
- heart-shaped biscuit (cookie) cutter
- small brush
- small fluted carnation cutter
- cocktail stick
- pink food-colouring pen

STORING

The cake can be made up to two days in advance, wrapped in foil and stored in an airtight container. The finished cake, covered in sugarpaste (fondant), can be stored for three to four days in a cool, dry place.

FREEZING

The un-iced cake can be frozen for up to three months.

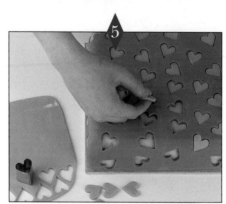

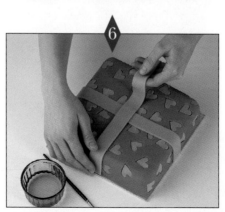

1 Preheat the oven to 180°C/350°F/Gas 4. Grease and line the base and sides of a 23 cm/9 in cake tin (pan). Spoon the mixture into the prepared tin (pan) and smooth the surface with a plastic spatula. Bake in the preheated oven for 1¼–1½ hours, or until a skewer inserted into the centre of the cake comes out clean. Leave for 5 minutes before turning out onto a wire rack to cool.

2 Cut the cake in half horizontally and spread with the vanilla butter icing. Sandwich with the top sponge cake and place the cake in the centre of the cakeboard. Brush the cake with apricot glaze. Lightly dust the work surface with icing (confectioners') sugar and roll out the marzipan to about ½ cm/¼ in thick. Use to cover the cake.

3 Colour 575 g/1¼ lb/1¼ lb sugarpaste (fondant) icing purple. Roll out the purple sugarpaste (fondant) on the work surface, lightly dusted with icing (confectioners') sugar. Use to cover the cake, smoothing down the sides gently and trimming away any excess sugarpaste (fondant).

4 Using the heart-shaped cutter, stamp out hearts all over the cake to make an even pattern. Remove the purple hearts with a small, sharp knife, taking care not to damage the surrounding sugarpaste (fondant). Knead the hearts together and keep this reserved purple sugarpaste (fondant) in a plastic bag to use later.

5 Colour 275 g/10 oz/10 oz sugarpaste (fondant) icing pink. Roll out to about ½ cm/¼ in thick on a work surface, lightly dusted with icing (confectioners') sugar. Use the heart-shaped cutter to cut out as many hearts as you need to fill the spaces left by the purple ones on the cake, re-rolling the pink sugarpaste (fondant), as necessary. Reserve the excess. Carefully insert the pink hearts into the spaces.

6 Roll out the reserved pink sugarpaste (fondant) to about ½ cm/¼ in thick on a work surface, lightly dusted with icing (confectioners') sugar and cut into three strips about 2 cm/¾ in wide and 30 cm/12 in long. Lay one strip across the centre of the cake and another at right angles across the centre, brushing the strips with a little water to secure. Trim away any excess sugarpaste (fondant) at the edges, if necessary. Reserve all the trimmings.

7 To make the bow, divide the remaining strip of pink sugarpaste (fondant) icing into quarters. Loop two of the quarters and seal the joins with a little water. Position at the centre of the cake, where the strips cross. Trim the ends of the remaining quarters to look like the ends of bows and overlap them across the joining of the loops; secure with a little water. Reserve the trimmings.

8 To make the flowers, roll out the remaining purple and pink sugarpaste (fondant) on a work surface, lightly dusted with icing (confectioners') sugar. Cut out two ½ cm/¼ in thick fluted rounds from each colour, using the carnation cutter.

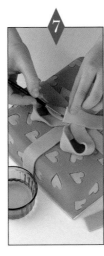

9 With a cocktail stick or toothpick, carefully roll out the edges of each fluted round to make the frilled petals. Use a little of the purple sugarpaste (fondant) to make two tiny balls for the centres of the flowers. Then, using a little water, place a pink flower on top of a purple one and the tiny ball in the centre. Carefully lift and pinch behind the flower to secure. Repeat with the other flower and position them both on the cake. Mould together any remaining sugarpaste (fondant), roll out and cut into a pretty tag. Write a name or short message using the food-colouring pen and position on the cake.

SAILING BOAT

Make this cake for someone who loves sailing or is going on a journey – you can even personalize the cake with a rice paper nametag flag, written with a food-colouring pen.

INGREDIENTS

Serves 10–12
- 3-egg quantity quick-mix sponge cake
- 60 ml/4 tbsp/4 tbsp apricot glaze
- 450 g/1 lb/1 lb sugarpaste (fondant) icing
- 1 grissini (bread stick)
- 1 sheet of rice paper
- 9 short candy sticks
- 4 Polo (Lifesaver) mints
- 1 thin red 'bootlace' liquorice strip
- 1 thin black 'bootlace' liquorice strip
- 1 black liquorice Catherine wheel, with an orange sweet in the centre
- 1 blue sherbet 'flying saucer'
- 350 g/12 oz/³⁄₄ lb butter icing coloured blue
- blue food colouring

MATERIALS AND EQUIPMENT

- 900 g/2 lb/5 cup loaf tin (bread pan)
- greaseproof (wax) paper
- 33 × 18 cm/13 × 7 in cakeboard
- 1 cocktail stick or toothpick
- black food-colouring pen

STORING

The cake can be made up to two days in advance, wrapped in foil and stored in an airtight container. The finished cake, covered in sugarpaste (fondant), can be stored for three to four days in a cool, dry place.

FREEZING

The un-iced cake can be frozen for up to three months.

VARIATION

To make this boat even more colourful, draw an attractive design on the sails using coloured pens. Remember that only the special cake decorating pens contain edible inks, so if you use another type of pen, don't eat the sails.

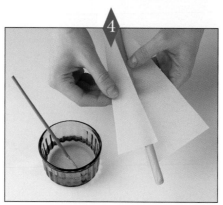

1 Preheat the oven to 180°C/350°F/Gas 4. Grease and line the base and sides of a 900 g/2 lb/5 cup loaf tin (bread pan). Spoon the cake mixture into the prepared tin (pan) and smooth the top with a plastic spatula. Bake in the preheated oven for 55–60 minutes, or until a skewer inserted into the centre of the cake comes out clean. Leave for 5 minutes before turning out on to a wire rack to cool.

2 Slice a thin layer off the top of the cake to make it perfectly flat. Trim one end to make a pointed bow. Using a small sharp knife, cut a shallow hollow from the centre of the cake, leaving a 1 cm/½ in border.

3 Brush the cake all over with the apricot glaze. Roll out the sugarpaste (fondant) icing to 35 × 23 cm/14 × 9 in rectangle and lay over the cake. Gently ease the sugarpaste (fondant) into the hollow middle and down the sides of the cake, until completely and evenly covered. Trim the edges at the base.

4 Cover the cakeboard with the blue butter icing, peaking it to resemble a rough sea. Position the cake on the iced board. Cut the rice paper into two tall triangular sails. Using a small brush, apply a little water along the length of the grissini (bread) stick and secure the rice paper sails to it. Insert the mast into the front of the hollowed compartment at the bow of the boat, pushing through the cake to the board.

5 Insert seven of the short candy sticks around the bow of the boat, leaving a little space between each one and allowing them to stand about 2.5 cm/1 in above the surface of the cake. Insert the remaining two short candy sticks at either side of the stern of the boat and hang two Polo (Lifesaver) mints on each, for the life belts. Use the bootlace liquorice strips to tie loosely in and out of the candy sticks at the bow of the boat for the guard rail. Trim away any excess, if necessary.

6 *Cut a small flag shape from the remaining rice paper and personalize it using the food colour pen. Stick onto the cocktail stick using a little water and position the flag at the stern of the boat.*

7 *Uncoil the liquorice Catherine wheel and remove the sweet from the centre. Use the liquorice to make a fender all around the outside of the boat, securing it with a little water. Trim the excess and use the remainder to line the seating area in the same way. Position the sweet from the centre of the Catherine wheel to one side of the boat for the searchlight. Place the sherbet flying saucer in the seating area for the cushion.*

SHIRT AND TIE CAKE

Instead of buying the man in your life yet another shirt and tie for his birthday, make him a cake for a deliciously novel surprise!

INGREDIENTS

Serves 20–30

- 4-egg quantity coffee-flavoured quick-mix sponge cake
- 350 g/12 oz/³⁄₄ lb coffee-flavoured butter icing
- 90 ml/6 tbsp/6 tbsp apricot glaze
- icing (confectioners') sugar, for dusting
- good 1 kg/2 lb 6 oz/2 lb 6 oz sugarpaste (fondant) icing
- blue food colouring
- 125 g/4 oz/1 cup icing (confectioners') sugar, sifted
- 45–60 ml/3–4 tbsp/3–4 tbsp water

MATERIALS AND EQUIPMENT

- 19 × 26.5 cm/7¹⁄₂ × 10¹⁄₂ in roasting tin (pan)
- greaseproof (wax) paper
- 30 × 32.5 cm/12 × 13 in cakeboard
- steel ruler
- wooden skewer
- piping bag fitted with a small round nozzle
- 40 × 5 cm/16 × 2 in piece of flexible card, the short ends cut at an angle, for the collar
- small brush
- 'Happy Birthday' cake decoration (optional)
- blue tissue paper (optional)

STORING

The cake can be made up to two days in advance, wrapped in foil and stored in an airtight container. The finished cake, covered in sugarpaste (fondant), can be stored for three to four days in a cool, dry place.

FREEZING

The un-iced cake can be frozen for up to three months.

VARIATION

Choose your own colour contrasts for the shirt and the tie to suit the man; for example, a blue or red collar on a white or red shirt with a zany yellow tie!

1 Preheat the oven to 180°C/350°F/Gas 4. Grease and line the base and sides of a 19 × 26.5 cm/7¹⁄₂ × 10¹⁄₂ in roasting tin (pan). Spoon the mixture into the prepared tin (pan) and smooth the surface with a plastic spatula. Bake in the preheated oven for 1¹⁄₄–1¹⁄₂ hours, or until a skewer inserted into the centre of the cake comes out clean. Leave for 5 minutes before turning out on to a wire rack to cool.

2 Cut the cake in half horizontally and spread with the coffee-flavoured butter icing. Sandwich together with the top half of the sponge cake. Brush the cake evenly with the apricot glaze and lightly dust the work surface with icing (confectioners') sugar. Colour 675 g/1¹⁄₂ lb/1¹⁄₂ lb sugar-paste (fondant) icing light blue. Roll out the light blue sugarpaste (fondant) to about 5 mm/¹⁄₄ in thick and use to cover the cake, gently easing the sugarpaste (fondant) down the sides and corners. Trim away any excess icing. Place the cake on the cakeboard.

3 Using a steel ruler, make grooves down the length and sides of the cake, in straight lines, about 2.5 cm/1 in apart. Use a wooden skewer to re-indent the grooves, rolling the skewer slightly from side to side to make the channels deeper and slightly wider.

4 Mix the icing (confectioners') sugar and water together in a small bowl to make a just thick glacé icing and use to fill the piping bag fitted with the small, round nozzle. Pipe lines of glacé icing into the grooves on the top and sides of the cake, moving slowly and evenly for the best results.

5 To make the collar, roll out 225 g/
8 oz/½ lb sugarpaste (fondant) icing,
on a work surface lightly dusted with icing
(confectioners') sugar, to a 40.5 × 10 cm/
16½ × 4 in rectangle. Lay the piece of
card for the collar on top, placing it along
one edge of the sugarpaste (fondant). Brush
a little water around the edges of the
sugarpaste (fondant), then carefully lift the
other edge of the sugarpaste (fondant) and
fold over the card to encase it completely.
Trim the two short ends to match the angles
of the card. Carefully lift the collar and
gently bend it round and position on the
cake, applying a little water to help secure it
in place.

6 Colour 175 g/6 oz/6 oz sugarpaste
(fondant) icing dark blue. To make the
tie, cut off one-third of the dark blue
sugarpaste (fondant) and shape into a
pyramid for the tie knot. Position the knot.
Lightly dust the work surface with icing
(confectioners') sugar and roll out the
remaining dark blue sugarpaste (fondant)
icing to about 5 mm/¼ in thick. Cut out a
tie piece to fit under the knot and long
enough to hang over the edge of the cake,
making it slightly wider at the end where
you cut a point. Position the tie piece,
tucking it under the knot and applying a
little water to secure it in place. Finish the
cake with the 'Happy Birthday' decoration
and tissue paper, if using.

MERRY-GO-ROUND CAKE

Choose your own figures to sit on the merry-go-round, from chocolate animals to jelly bears.

Remember to position the top of the merry-go-round at the last minute for the best results.

INGREDIENTS

Serves 16–20

- 3-egg quantity lemon-flavoured quick-mix sponge cake
- 60 ml/4 tbsp/4 tbsp apricot glaze
- icing (confectioners') sugar, to dust
- 575 g/1¼ lb/1¼ lb sugarpaste (fondant) icing
- orange and yellow food colouring
- 8 × 18 cm/7 in long candy sticks
- sweet (candy) figures

MATERIALS AND EQUIPMENT

- 2 × 20 cm/8 in round sandwich cake tins (pans)
- greaseproof (wax) paper
- 23 cm/9 in round fluted cakeboard
- 18 cm/7 in round piece of stiff card
- cocktail stick or toothpick
- 2 different sizes of star-shaped biscuit (cookie) cutters

STORING

The cake can be made up to two days in advance, wrapped in foil and stored in an airtight container. The finished cake, covered in sugarpaste (fondant), can be stored for three to four days in a cool, dry place.

FREEZING

The un-iced cake can be frozen for up to three months.

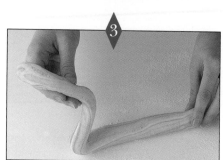

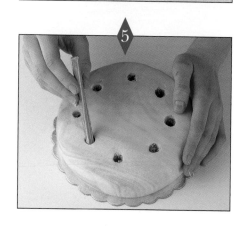

1 Preheat the oven to 180°C/350°F/Gas 4. Grease and line the bases of two 20 cm/8 in round sandwich tins (pans). Spoon two-thirds of the mixture into one tin (pan) and the other third into the other tin (pan). Smooth the surfaces with a plastic spatula. Bake for 55–60 minutes, or until a skewer inserted into the centre of each cake comes out clean. Leave for 5 minutes before turning out onto a wire rack to cool.

2 Place the larger cake, upside-down, on the fluted cakeboard to make the base of the merry-go-round, and place the smaller cake, right-side up, on the piece of card. Brush both cakes evenly with the apricot glaze and set aside. Lightly dust the work surface with icing (confectioners') sugar and place 450 g/1 lb/1 lb sugarpaste (fondant) icing on it. Using the cocktail stick or toothpick, apply a few spots of the orange food colouring to the sugarpaste (fondant).

3 To achieve the marbled effect in the sugarpaste (fondant) icing, roll into a sausage shape on the work surface. Fold the sausage shape in half and continue to roll out until it reaches its original length. Fold over again and roll out again into a sausage shape. Continue this process until the fondant is streaked with the orange colour.

4 Divide the marbled sugarpaste (fondant) into two-thirds and one third. Roll out the larger portion on the work surface lightly dusted with icing (confectioners') sugar and use to cover the larger cake. Repeat with the smaller portion of marbled sugarpaste (fondant) and use to cover the smaller cake. Trim away any excess sugarpaste (fondant) and reserve, wrapped in cling film (plastic wrap).

5 Using one of the candy sticks, make eight holes at even distances around the edge of the larger cake, leaving about a 2 cm/¾ in border. Press the upright stick right through the cake to the board. Knead the reserved marbled sugarpaste (fondant) until the orange colour is evenly blended, then roll out on the work surface lightly dusted with icing (confectioners') sugar. Using the smaller star cutter, cut out nine stars. Cover with cling film (plastic wrap) and set aside. Colour 125 g/4 oz/¼ lb sugarpaste (fondant) icing yellow. Roll out on a surface lightly dusted with icing (confectioners') sugar and cut out nine stars with the larger star cutter. Sit the smaller cake on an upturned bowl and stick eight larger and eight smaller stars around the edge of the cake, using a little water to secure. Stick the remaining stars on top of the cake.

6 To secure the sweet figures to the candy sticks, stick tiny balls of the excess sugarpaste (fondant) behind the figures and then lightly press onto the sticks. Leave to set for about 30 minutes. Place the candy sticks in the holes on the larger cake.

7 To assemble the cake, carefully lift the smaller cake, with its card base, onto the candy sticks, making sure it balances before letting go!

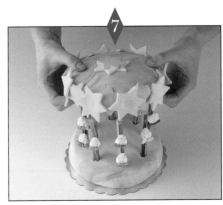

MOBILE PHONE CAKE

Mobile phones keep getting smaller, but rest assured this delicious cake is a decent size!

INGREDIENTS

Serves 8–10
- 2-egg quantity vanilla-flavoured quick-mix sponge cake
- 30 ml/2 tbsp/2 tbsp apricot glaze
- icing (confectioners') sugar, for dusting
- 375 g/13 oz/13 oz sugarpaste (fondant) icing
- black food colouring
- 10 small square sweets (candies)
- 1–2 stripey liquorice sweets (candies)
- 30–45 ml/2–3 tbsp/2–3 tbsp icing (confectioners') sugar
- 2.5–5 ml/½–1 tsp/½–1 tsp water

MATERIALS AND EQUIPMENT

- 900 g/2 lb/5 cup loaf tin (bread pan)
- 23 × 18 cm/9 × 7 in cakeboard
- diamond-shaped biscuit (cookie) cutter
- small brush
- small strip of kitchen foil
- piping bag fitted with a small round nozzle

STORING

The cake can be made up to two days in advance, wrapped in foil and stored in an airtight container. The finished cake, covered in sugarpaste (fondant), can be stored for three to four days in a cool, dry place.

FREEZING

The un-iced cake can be frozen for up to three months.

1 Preheat the oven to 180°C/350°F/Gas 4. Grease and line the base and sides of a 900 g/2 lb/5 cup loaf tin (bread pan). Spoon the mixture into the prepared tin (pan) and smooth the surface with a plastic spatula. Bake in the preheated oven for 40–50 minutes, or until a skewer inserted into the centre of the cake comes out clean. Leave for 5 minutes before turning out on to a wire rack to cool.

2 Turn the cake upside-down and starting about 2.5 cm/1 in along the cake, slice into it, across and at an angle, about 1 cm/½ in deep. Cut out this wedge, then slice horizontally along the length of the cake, stopping about 2.5 cm/1 in away from the end. Withdraw the knife and re-insert it at the end of the cake and slice into the cake to meet up with the horizontal cut. Remove the inner piece of cake and discard.

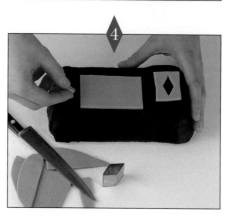

3 Place the cake on the cakeboard. Brush the cake evenly with the apricot glaze. Colour 275 g/10 oz/10 oz sugarpaste (fondant) icing black. Lightly dust the work surface with icing (confectioners') sugar and roll out the black sugarpaste (fondant) to about 5 mm/¼ in thick. Use to cover the cake, carefully smoothing the sugarpaste (fondant) into the carved shape of the cake and down the sides and corners. Trim away any excess sugarpaste (fondant) and reserve, wrapped in cling film (plastic wrap).

4 Colour 75 g/3 oz/3 oz sugarpaste (fondant) icing grey, with a little black food colouring. Roll out the grey sugarpaste (fondant) to about 5 mm/¼ in thick on a work surface lightly dusted with icing (confectioners') sugar. Cut out one piece of sugarpaste (fondant) to fit the centre of the cake, leaving a 1 cm/½ in border and another piece, about 2.5 cm/1 in square. Using the diamond-shaped biscuit (cookie) cutter, stamp out the centre of the square. Place the diamond at the bottom of the phone, and the square at the top. Position the piece of sugarpaste (fondant) for the centre, securing all the grey pieces with a small brush dipped in a little water.

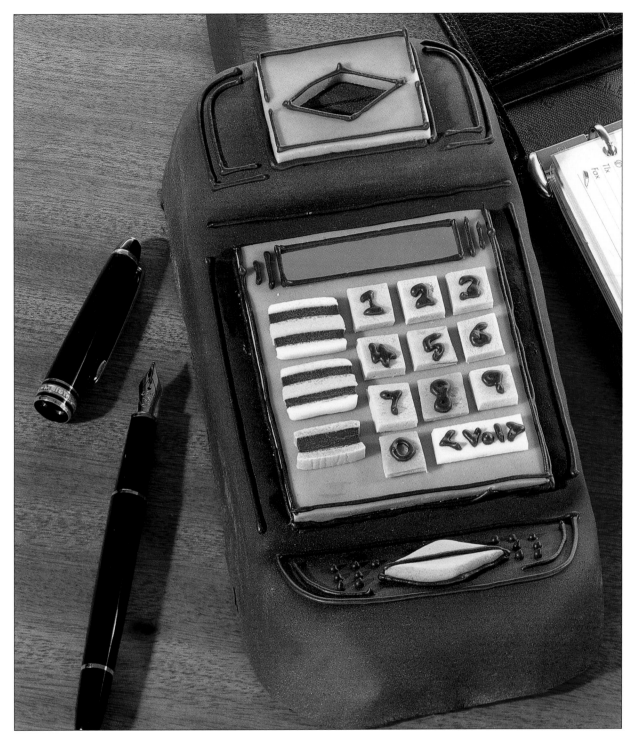

5 *Position the sweets (candies) and the strip of kitchen foil for the dial pad. To make the glacé icing, mix the icing (confectioners') sugar with the water and black food colouring, until of piping consistency. Fill the piping bag fitted with the small, round nozzle and pipe border lines around the edges of the phone, including the grey pieces of sugarpaste (fondant). Pipe the numbers on the keys.*

6 *Knead the reserved black sugarpaste (fondant) and use to roll into a sausage shape for the aerial. Indent the top with a knife and position at the top of the phone, to one side. Secure with a little water.*

RAINBOW SNAKE CAKE

This wild cake needs no cooking. It uses leftover sponge-cake crumbs – or you can buy a sponge cake and grind it yourself. Its heavy texture and sweet flavour make it an excellent party cake, for kids or adults. You only need serve a little, so it goes a long way. For a large party, double the ingredients to make an extra big snake. Use rubber gloves to protect your hands when colouring the marzipan and remember to wash them between colours.

INGREDIENTS

Serves 10–15
- 175 g/6 oz/3 cups plain sponge-cake crumbs
- 175 g/6 oz/1½ cups ground almonds
- 75 g/3 oz/6 tbsp light brown muscovado (molasses) sugar
- 5 ml/1 tsp/1 tsp ground mixed spice
- 2.5 ml/½ tsp/½ tsp ground cinnamon
- 45 ml/3 tbsp/3 tbsp fresh orange juice
- finely grated zest of 1 orange
- 75 ml/5 tbsp/5 tbsp clear runny honey or golden syrup (light corn syrup)
- 675 g/1½ lb/1½ lb white commercial or homemade marzipan
- icing (confectioners') sugar, for dusting
- red, yellow, orange, violet and green food colouring
- 2 red sugar-coated chocolate Smarties (M&Ms)
- 125 g/4 oz/2 cups desiccated (dry unsweetened shredded) coconut
- wine-gum (chewy) snake sweets (optional)

MATERIALS AND EQUIPMENT

- 5 cocktail sticks (or toothpicks)
- rolling pin
- 25 cm/10 in round cakeboard
- small piece of thin red card cut into a tongue shape
- small star-shaped cutter
- small brush

STORING

The marzipan-iced cake can be made up to four days in advance and stored in an airtight container in a cool, dry place.

FREEZING

Not recommended.

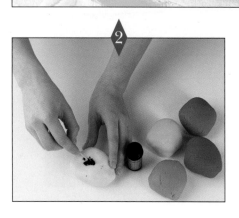

1 In a large mixing bowl, combine the cake crumbs, almonds, sugar, spices, orange juice and zest and the honey. Stir well until all the ingredients hold together in a moist, thick paste. Set aside.

2 To colour the marzipan, divide it into five equal portions. Lightly dust the work surface with icing (confectioners') sugar and apply one of the food colourings to one of the portions of marzipan, using a cocktail stick or toothpick. Knead the colour into the marzipan, until evenly blended. Clean the work surface and lightly dust again with icing (confectioners') sugar. Take another piece of marzipan and apply another of the colourings. Repeat this process, until all five portions of marzipan are different colours, using a new cocktail stick (toothpick) each time. Remove a tiny ball from the green portion and reserve, covered in cling film (plastic wrap).

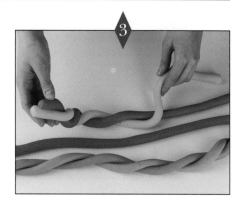

3 Using your hands, roll each piece of marzipan out on a work surface lightly dusted with icing (confectioners') sugar, to a sausage shape, about 1 cm/½ in in diameter. Line up the sausage shapes next to each other on the work surface and twist together the two outside sausages, leaving only the centre sausage untouched. Push the two outside twists together to squeeze against the middle sausage firmly.

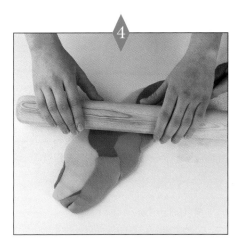

4 Use a little icing (confectioners') sugar to dust the rolling pin and make short, sharp downward movements starting at one end, rolling the marzipan out a little at a time to about 15 cm/6 in wide. Keep the rolled width even all along the snake. Carefully slide a heavy, sharp knife underneath the rolled out marzipan to unstick it from the work surface. Flip the rolled out marzipan over, taking care not to tear it.

5 Spoon the cake-crumb mixture evenly down the centre of the marzipan, using your hands to form it into a firm sausage shape. Starting at one end, gather up the sides of the marzipan around the cake mixture, pinching the sides together firmly to seal, until the cake mixture is completely encased. Shape the head by flattening the marzipan slightly, and the tail by squeezing it into a tapered end. Roll the snake over so the seal lies underneath.

6 Carefully slide the snake on to the cakeboard, tail-end first, coiling it round as you go. The head can either be propped up on an extra lump of marzipan or left to flop over the rest of the snake. Both methods look very effective. Make a small incision where the mouth would be and insert the red tongue. Roll the reserved green marzipan out on a work surface lightly dusted with icing (confectioners') sugar and cut out two eyes, using the small star cutter. Position the eyes, securing them with a small brush dipped in a little water. Press the small Smarties or M&Ms on top.

7 Place the desiccated (dry unsweetened shredded) coconut in a bowl and add a few spots of green food colouring with a little water. Stir until the coconut is flecked green. Scatter around the snake on the board to make the grass. Decorate with the wine-gum (chewy candy) snakes, if using.

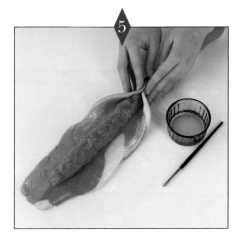

EASTER CAKE

An unusual presentation for a spicy Easter fruit cake. The cake is covered with marzipan and chocolate moulding icing, then finished with ribbons and eggs made from chocolate modelling paste. The cake can be completed up to four weeks in advance.

INGREDIENTS

Serves 16

- 125 g/4 oz/½ cup softened butter or margarine
- 125 g/4 oz/½ cup light brown sugar
- 3 eggs
- 175 g/6 oz/1½ cups plain (all-purpose) flour
- 10 ml/2 tsp/2 tsp ground mixed spice
- 400 g/14 oz/3½ cups mixed dried fruit
- 50 g/2 oz/¼ cup glacé cherries, chopped
- 50 g/2 oz/¼ cup hazelnuts
- 45 ml/3 tbsp/3 tbsp apricot glaze
- 450 g/1 lb/1 lb homemade or commercial marzipan
- brown food colouring

MATERIALS AND EQUIPMENT

- 1.5 l/2½ pt/3 pt pudding basin (bowl)
- greaseproof (wax) paper
- 25 cm/10 in round gold cakeboard
- clean piece sponge
- several squares of gold foil, about 6.5 cm/2½ in in diameter
- paintbrush

STORING

The iced cake can be covered loosely in foil and stored in a cool dry place for up to four weeks.

FREEZING

The fruit cake can be frozen for up to six months.

CHOCOLATE MOULDING ICING

- 100 g/4 oz/4 squares plain (semisweet) or milk chocolate
- 30 ml/2 tbsp/2 tbsp liquid glucose
- 1 egg white
- 450 g/1 lb/3½ cups icing (confectioners') sugar
- cornflour (cornstarch) for dusting

CHOCOLATE MODELLING PASTE

- 50 g/2 oz/2 squares plain chocolate
- 50 g/2 oz/2 squares white chocolate
- 30 ml/2 tbsp/2 tbsp liquid glucose
- pink paste food colouring

1 Preheat the oven to 150°C/300°F/Gas 2. Grease and line the base of the pudding basin (bowl) with a circle of greaseproof (wax) paper. Cream together the butter or margarine and brown sugar. Gradually add the eggs with a little of the flour to prevent curdling. Sieve (sift) the remaining flour and spice and add to the bowl. Stir in the mixed fruit and nuts and turn into the prepared basin or bowl. Level the surface and bake for 1½ hours or until a skewer inserted into the centre of the cake comes out clean. Allow to cool completely.

2 To make the chocolate moulding icing, break up the chocolate and place in a bowl with the glucose over a pan of hot water. Leave until melted, cool slightly then add the egg white. Gradually add the icing (confectioners') sugar, beating well after each addition, until too stiff to manage. Turn out onto a flat surface and knead in the remaining sugar until stiff.

3 To make the modelling paste, melt the plain (semisweet) and white chocolate in separate bowls. Add half the glucose to the plain chocolate and stir until a stiff paste is formed. Wrap tightly. Add some pink food colouring and the remaining glucose to the white chocolate and mix to a paste. Chill both pastes until firm.

4 Cut a triangular wedge out of the cake, place the cake on the board and brush all over with apricot glaze. Roll out the marzipan on a surface dusted with icing (confectioners') sugar and cover the cake, tucking the paste into the cut section to maintain the cut-out shape. Trim off the excess marzipan around the base.

5 Roll out the chocolate moulding icing on a surface dusted with cornflour (cornstarch) and use to cover the cake in the same way. Cut two thin strips from the marzipan trimmings. Dampen the undersides with water and position them inside the cut-out wedge to resemble a marzipan layer.

6 Thin a little brown food colouring with water. Dip the sponge in the colour and stipple the surface of the icing. Leave to dry.

7 Lightly knead two-thirds of the modelling paste and shape into 18 small eggs. Cover some with gold foil. Position the eggs inside the cut-out wedge.

Thinly roll out the remaining modelling paste and cut 2 cm/¾ in wide strips from the dark paste and 5 mm/¼ in wide strips from the pink paste. Dampen the undersides of the pink paste and lay over the dark. Cut two 13 cm/5 in strips, press the ends together to make loops and secure to the cake. Secure two 7.5 cm/3 in strips for ribbon ends and cover the centre with another small strip. (Place a piece of crumpled foil under each strip until hardened.)

GHOST

This children's cake is really simple to make yet very effective. Use an 18 cm/7 in square cake of your choice, such as a citrus- or chocolate-flavoured Madeira, or a light fruit cake.

INGREDIENTS

Serves 14

- 4-egg quantity orange-flavoured quick-mix sponge cake
- 900 g/2 lb/2 lb sugarpaste (fondant) icing
- black food colouring
- 350 g/12 oz/³/₄ lb butter icing
- cornflour (cornstarch) for dusting

MATERIALS AND EQUIPMENT

- 18 cm/7 in square cake tin (pan)
- greaseproof (wax) paper
- 300 ml/½ pt/1¼ cup pudding basin (bowl)
- 23 cm/9 in round cakeboard
- palette knife (spatula)
- fine paintbrush

STORING

The iced cake can be covered loosely in foil and stored in a cool, dry place for up to two weeks.

FREEZING

The sponge can be frozen for up to two months.

1 Preheat the oven to 150°C/300°F/Gas 2. Grease and line the base of cake tin with greased greaseproof (wax) paper. Grease and line the base of pudding basin (bowl) with greaseproof (wax) paper. Half-fill the basin with cake mixture and turn the remainder into the cake tin (pan). Bake the basin for 25 minutes and the tin for 1½ hours. Allow to cool.

2 Knead a little black food colouring into 125 g/4 oz/¼ lb of the sugarpaste (fondant) icing and use to cover the cakeboard. Trim off the excess.

3 Cut two small corners off the large cake. Cut two larger wedges off the other two corners. Stand the large cake on the iced board. Halve the larger cake trimmings and wedge around the base of cake.

4 Secure the small cake to the top of the larger cake with a little of the butter icing. Use the remaining butter icing to completely cover the cake.

5 Roll out the remaining sugarpaste (fondant) on a surface dusted with cornflour (cornstarch) to an oval shape about 51 cm/20 in long and 30 cm/12 in wide. Lay over the cake, letting the icing fall into folds around sides. Gently smooth the icing over the top half of the cake and trim off any excess around the base.

6 Using black food colouring and a fine paintbrush, paint two oval eyes onto the head.

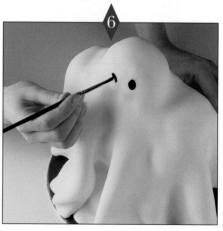

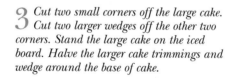

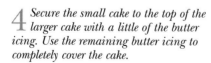

BIRTHDAY BALLOONS

A colourful cake for a child's birthday party, made using either a round sponge cake or fruit cake base.

INGREDIENTS

Serves 18–20

- 20 cm/8 in round sponge or fruit cake, covered with 800 g/1¾ lb/ 1¾ lb marzipan, if liked
- 900 g/2 lb/2 lb sugarpaste (fondant) icing
- red, green and yellow food colourings
- cornflour (cornstarch), for dusting
- 3 eggs
- 2 egg whites
- 450 g/1 lb/4 cups icing (confectioners') sugar

MATERIALS AND EQUIPMENT

- 25 cm/10 in round silver cakecard
- 3 bamboo skewers, 25 cm/10 in, 24 cm/9½ in and 23 cm/9 in long
- small star cutter
- baking parchment
- greaseproof (wax) paper piping bags
- fine writing nozzle
- 1 m/1 yd fine coloured ribbon
- birthday candles

STORING

The iced cake will keep well in a cool place for up to three weeks.

FREEZING

A fruit cake base can be frozen for up to six months, and a sponge base for up to two months.

Template for the balloon-shaped run-outs; reproduced at about actual size.

1 Place the cake on the cakecard. Colour 50 g/2 oz/2 oz of the sugarpaste (fondant) red, 50 g/2 oz/2 oz green and 125 g/4 oz/¼ lb yellow. Roll out the remaining icing on a surface dusted with cornflour (cornstarch) and use to cover the cake. Use 50 g/2 oz/2 oz of the yellow icing to cover the cakecard.

2 Using the tip of a skewer or the end of a paintbrush, make a small hole in the pointed end of one egg. Stir the egg lightly inside then tip out into a bowl. Repeat with the remaining eggs. Carefully wash and dry the shells. (The eggs should be strained before using.)

3 Roll out the red sugarpaste (fondant) icing to about 11 cm/4½ in diameter circle and use to cover one of the egg shells, smoothing to fit around sides and trimming off any excess around the pointed ends. Keep smoothing the icing in the palms of the hands. Push a bamboo skewer up through hole and rest in a tall glass to harden. Repeat on other egg shells with the green and yellow sugarpaste (fondant).

4 Roll out the red, green and yellow trimmings and cut out a small star shape from each. Dampen lightly then thread onto the skewers and secure to the bases of balloons, matching the colours, for the balloon knots.

5 Trace 16 balloon shapes onto a large sheet of baking parchment. Beat the egg whites with the icing (confectioners') sugar until smooth and divide among 4 bowls. Add red colouring to one bowl, green to the second and yellow to the third, leaving the last white. Cover each tightly with cling film (plastic wrap) to prevent a crust forming.

6 Place the white icing in a piping bag fitted with a plain writing nozzle and use to pipe over the traced outlines. Leave to harden slightly. Thin the green icing with a little water until the consistency of pouring cream. Place in a greaseproof (wax) paper piping bag and snip off end. Use to fill a third of the balloon shapes. Repeat with the red and yellow icings. Leave the run-outs for at least 24 hours to harden.

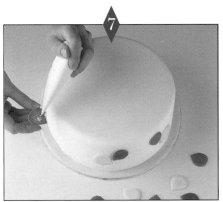

7 Carefully peel the balloons off the
baking parchment and secure around
the sides of the cake. Pipe strings for the
balloons with white icing.

8 Press the large balloons into the top of
cake and decorate with the ribbon.
Press the candles into the icing around the
top edge.

FISH

A very easy, but colourful cake, perfect for a small child's birthday party. Candles can be pressed into the icing covering the board.

INGREDIENTS

Serves 8
- 2-egg quantity quick-mix sponge cake
- 450 g/1 lb/1 lb sugarpaste (fondant) icing
- blue, orange, red, mauve and green food colourings
- cornflour (cornstarch), for dusting
- 350 g/12 oz/³/₄ lb butter icing
- 1 blue Smartie (M&M)

MATERIALS AND EQUIPMENT

- 3.4 l/6 pt/7½ pt ovenproof mixing bowl
- large oval cakecard or board
- palette knife (spatula)
- 2.5 cm/1 in plain biscuit (cookie) cutter
- greaseproof (wax) paper piping bag

STORING

The iced cake can be covered loosely in foil and stored for up to one week.

FREEZING

The sponge cake can be frozen for up to two months.

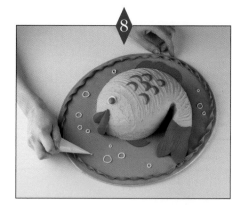

1 *Preheat the oven to 170°C/325°F/Gas 3. Grease and line base of the mixing bowl with a circle of greaseproof (wax) paper. Spoon the cake mixture into the prepared bowl, level the surface and bake for 40–50 minutes until just firm, or until a skewer inserted into the middle of the cake comes out clean. Allow to cool.*

2 *Colour two-thirds of the sugarpaste (fondant) icing blue and roll out very thinly on a surface dusted with cornflour (cornstarch). Lightly dampen the cakecard or board and cover with the sugarpaste (fondant) icing. Trim off excess icing.*

3 *Invert the cake onto a flat surface and trim to create a fish shape with a curved tail. Using a small knife, trim the edges to give sloping sides. Place on the icing-*

4 *Colour all but 15 ml/1 tbsp/1 tbsp of the butter icing orange. Cover the cake completely with the orange butter icing and smooth down with a palette knife (spatula). Score curved lines for scales with the palette knife (spatula), starting from the tail-end and working up towards head.*

5 *Colour half the remaining sugarpaste (fondant) red. Shape and position two lips. Thinly roll the remainder and cut out the tail and fins. Mark with lines using a knife and position on the fish.*

6 *Roll a small ball of white sugarpaste (fondant) icing, flatten slightly and position for the eye. Press the blue Smartie (M&M) into centre.*

7 *Colour a small ball of sugarpaste (fondant) mauve, cut out crescent-shaped scales using a biscuit (cookie) cutter and place on the fish. Colour the remaining sugarpaste (fondant) icing green, roll out and cut long thin strips. Twist each strip and arrange them around board.*

8 *Place the reserved butter icing in a piping bag and snip off the end. Pipe small circles on the cakeboard around fish for bubbles.*

CHRISTMAS CAKE

An unusual Christmas cake which is thoroughly enjoyable to make, provided that you like painting and have a reasonably steady hand.

INGREDIENTS

Serves 35
- 25 cm/10 in round rich fruit cake, covered with 1.1 kg/2½ lb/2½ lb marzipan
- 1.4 kg/3 lb/3 lb sugarpaste (fondant) icing
- cornflour (cornstarch), for dusting
- red, yellow, green and mauve food colourings

MATERIALS AND EQUIPMENT

- 33 cm/13 in round gold cakeboard
- baking parchment
- dressmakers' pins
- fine paintbrush
- 1 m/1 yd × 2.5 cm/1 in wide red ribbon
- red candle

STORING

The iced cake can be wrapped loosely in foil and stored in a cool place for up to one month.

FREEZING

The fruit cake base can be frozen for up to six months.

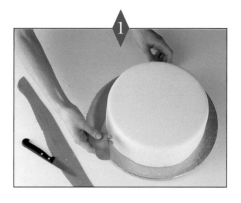

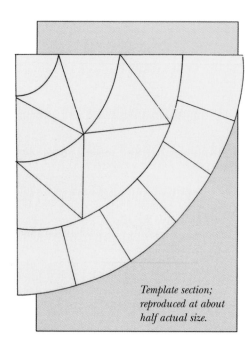

Template section; reproduced at about half actual size.

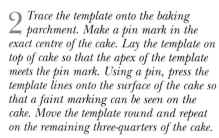

1 Place the cake on the board. Reserve 125 g/4 oz/¼ lb of the sugarpaste (fondant) icing and use the remainder to cover the cake. Colour the reserved sugarpaste (fondant) red and roll out thinly on a surface dusted with cornflour (cornstarch). Dampen the surface of the cakeboard and cover with strips of icing. Smooth down gently and trim off the excess around edge of board. Leave for at least 24 hours to harden.

2 Trace the template onto the baking parchment. Make a pin mark in the exact centre of the cake. Lay the template on top of cake so that the apex of the template meets the pin mark. Using a pin, press the template lines onto the surface of the cake so that a faint marking can be seen on the cake. Move the template round and repeat on the remaining three-quarters of the cake.

3 Cut another piece of baking parchment to fit around the circumference of cake and 6.5 cm/2½ in wide. Lay around the sides of the cake so that the base of the template rests on the cakeboard, securing the ends with a pin. Using a pin, mark a line onto the icing around the top edge of the template. Cut the template in half lengthways and reposition around the cake as before. Mark another line around the top edge of the template, halfway down the sides of the cake. Remove the template.

36

4 Place a little red, yellow, green and mauve food colourings onto a large flat plate and thin each with a little water, as if on a painter's palette. Paint a red triangle of icing onto the cake next to the central circle to within 1 mm/¹⁄₁₆ in of the template markings. Paint another triangle opposite the first. Fill in the centres with yellow. Use the green and mauve colours to fill the remaining triangles around the central circle.

5 Using a clean paintbrush dampened with water, lightly 'smudge' the red and yellow colours together. Repeat on the green and mauve triangles.

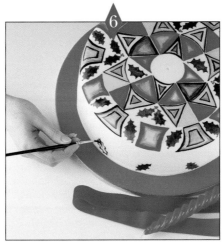

6 Using this technique, build up a design over the top and sides of the cake, creating a random design or following the photographed cake. Leave the area between the two marked lines around the cake blank for the ribbon. Incorporate a holly leaf at intervals around the cake, first painting an outline and then filling in with colour. Finish the leaves with red berries.

7 Secure the ribbon around cake and place a candle in the centre, using a little icing (confectioners') sugar mixed to a paste with water as glue.

ARTIST'S BOX AND PALETTE

Making cakes is an art in itself, and this cake proves it. It is the perfect celebration cake for any artist of any age.

INGREDIENTS

Serves 30
- 20 cm/8 in square rich fruit cake
- 45 ml/3 tbsp/3 tbsp apricot glaze
- 450 g/1 lb/1 lb marzipan
- 800 g/1¾ lb/1¾ lb sugarpaste (fondant) icing
- 125 g/4 oz/⅓ cup royal icing, for fixing
- chestnut, blue, mulberry, yellow, green, black, silver and paprika food colourings

MATERIALS AND EQUIPMENT

- stiff paper for template
- greaseproof (wax) paper
- 25–26 cm/10 in square cakeboard
- fine paintbrush

STORING

The iced cake can be stored in an airtight container for up to three weeks.

FREEZING

Not recommended.

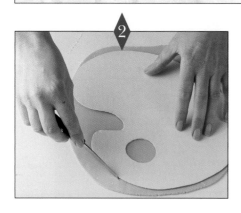

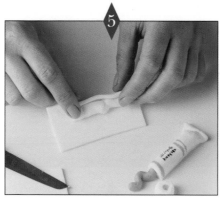

1 Brush the cake with the apricot glaze. Roll out the marzipan, cover the cake and leave to dry for 12 hours.

2 Make a template out of stiff paper in the shape of a painter's palette that will fit on top of the cake. Take 175 g/6 oz/6 oz sugarpaste (fondant) and colour a very pale chestnut. Roll out and cut out the palette shape using the template. Place on a sheet of greaseproof (wax) paper and leave to dry for 12 hours.

3 Take 450 g/1 lb/1 lb sugarpaste (fondant) icing and colour brown with the chestnut colouring. Roll this out, brush the marzipanned cake with a little water to slightly dampen, and cover the cake with the brown-coloured sugarpaste (fondant) icing, cutting away any surplus. Position the cake on the cakeboard, securing underneath with a dab of royal icing. Leave to dry for several hours.

4 Take the remaining 175 g/6 oz/6 oz of the sugarpaste (fondant) icing. Leave half white, divide the remainder into seven equal parts and colour yellow, blue, black, silver, paprika, green and mulberry. Shape the box handle and clips with black and silver and leave to dry on greaseproof (wax) paper for several hours. Shape the paintbrush bristles from paprika-coloured sugarpaste and mark the hairs of the bristles with a knife. Shape the paintbrush handles in various colours and attach the handles, silver metal parts and bristles with a little royal icing. Leave to dry on greaseproof (wax) paper for several hours.

5 Shape the paint tubes from small oblongs of white rolled-out sugarpaste (fondant) icing, sealing the edges with a little water.

6 Paint on markings with a fine paintbrush. Shape squeezed-out paint in various colours and attach two to the paint tubes with a little, royal icing. Leave all to dry on greaseproof (wax) paper for several hours.

7 Roll out two small rectangles of any remaining white sugarpaste (fondant) icing to represent sheets of paper, and with a paintbrush and watered down food colours, brush on patterns. Leave to dry on greaseproof (wax) paper for several hours.

8 *Using a fine paintbrush, paint wood markings onto the box.*

9 *To assemble, using a little royal icing, attach the handle and clips onto the front side of the box, and the palette to the top of the cake. Position the paintbrushes, paint tubes, squeezed-out paint and painted paper on the cake and around the board.*

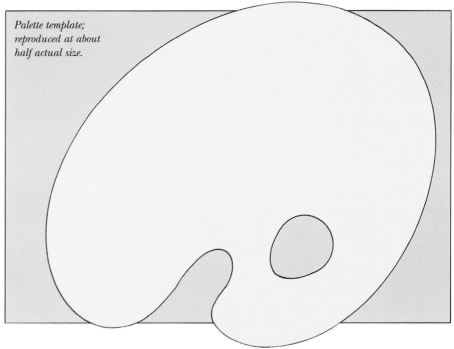

Palette template; reproduced at about half actual size.

LIQUORICE LOOKALIKE CAKE

If liquorice sweets (candies) are a favourite, then this is a cake to fantasize over. Larger than life size, its base is a square Madeira cake filled with butter icing, and topped with a pile of smaller lookalike liquorice sweets (candies).

INGREDIENTS

Serves 15–20
- 20 cm/8 in square Madeira cake
- 15 cm/6 in square Madeira cake
- 675 g/1½ lb/1½ lb butter icing
- 45 ml/3 tbsp/3 tbsp apricot glaze
- 350 g/12 oz/¾ lb marzipan
- 800 g/1¾ lb/1¾ lb sugarpaste (fondant) icing
- egg-yellow, black, blue, mulberry food colourings

MATERIALS AND EQUIPMENT

- 25 cm/10 in square cakeboard
- 4.5 cm/1¾ in round cutter

STORING

Kept in an airtight container, the cake will stay fresh for up to three days.

FREEZING

Not recommended.

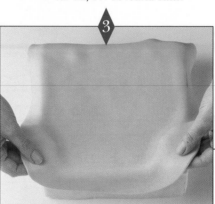

1 Cut both the cakes horizontally into three. Fill with the butter icing, reserving a little to coat the outsides of the smaller cake. Wrap and set aside the smaller cake.

2 Brush the 20 cm/8 in cake with the apricot glaze. Roll out the marzipan and cover the cake. Position the cake on the cakeboard, securing underneath with a little butter icing. Leave to dry for 12 hours.

3 Take 350 g/12 oz/¾ lb of the sugarpaste (fondant) and colour yellow. Take 125 g/4 oz/¼ lb of the sugarpaste (fondant) and colour half black and leave the other half white. Brush the marzipanned cake lightly with water. Roll out the yellow icing; cover the top and down one third of the sides of the cake.

4 Roll out the white icing to a strip wide and long enough to cover the sides of the bottom one-third of the cake. Position onto the cake, securing the join with a little water. Roll out the black icing to a strip wide enough and long enough to fill the central third strip, between the yellow and white strips. Position onto the cake.

5 Take the 15 cm/6 in cake. Cut into three equal strips. Divide two of the strips each into three squares. From the remaining strip cut out two circles (about 4.5 cm/1¾ in), using a cutter as a guide.

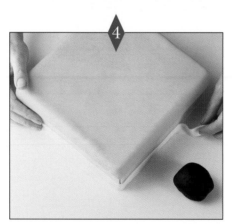

6 Take another 100 g/4 oz/¼ lb sugarpaste (fondant) and colour it black. Take the remaining 225 g/8 oz/½ lb sugarpaste (fondant) and divide into four equal amounts: colour blue, pink, yellow and leave one portion white.

7 Coat the outsides of the cut-out cake pieces with the reserved butter icing. Make the square liquorice sweets (candies) for the top of the cake using the coloured icings, rolling out strips for the sides and squares to coat the tops. Secure any of the strip joins with a little water.

8 Make small balls of pink and blue icing for the round sweets (candies), attaching them by lightly pressing into the butter icing.

9 To make the small rolls for the edges of the cake, roll out any black sugarpaste (fondant) trimmings into a strip about 18 × 13 cm/7 × 5 in. With your fingers, roll out 18 cm/7 in long sausage shapes of yellow, pink, white and blue icing. Position one of the colours down the length of the black strip, roll over to form a filled roll, securing the join underneath with water. Slice into three across. Repeat with the remaining colours.

10 Arrange the smaller liquorice allsorts in a pile on top and around the edges of the large cake.

CANDLE CAKE

Marbled icing is so effective that little other decoration is required. This design combines blue and orange but any other strong colour combination is equally effective.

INGREDIENTS

Serves 20
- 20 cm/8 in round rich fruit cake, covered with 800 g/1¾ lb/1¾ lb marzipan
- 900 g/2 lb/2 lb sugarpaste (fondant) icing
- blue, green and orange food colourings
- cornflour (cornstarch), for dusting

MATERIALS AND EQUIPMENT

- 25 cm/10 in round silver cakecard
- 1 bamboo skewer
- 2 household candles
- cling film (plastic wrap)

STORING

The iced cake can be wrapped loosely in foil and stored in a cool place for up to four weeks.

FREEZING

The fruit cake base can be frozen for up to six months.

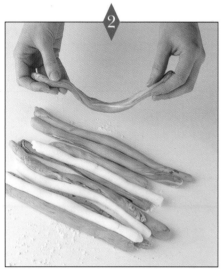

1 Place the cake on the card. Colour 125 g/4 oz/¼ lb of the sugarpaste (fondant) icing orange and reserve. Reserve another 125 g/4 oz/¼ lb of white sugarpaste (fondant). Divide the remaining icing into three parts. Knead the orange colouring into one piece until deep orange but still streaked with colour. Knead a mixture of blue and green colour into another piece until streaky. Leave the remaining piece white.

2 Lightly dust the work surface with the cornflour (cornstarch). Roll long sausages of icing in the three colours and lay on the work surface.

3 Twist the colours together and knead for several seconds until the strips of colour are secured together but retain their individual colours.

4 Roll out the marbled icing and use to cover the cake, trimming off the excess around the base.

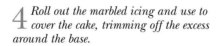

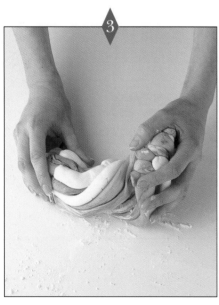

5 Take a small piece of the reserved orange sugarpaste (fondant), about the size of a large grape, and shape into a candle flame. Thread onto the end of the bamboo skewer. Thinly roll the remaining orange sugarpaste (fondant) and use to cover the card around cake. Re-roll the trimmings and cut another strip, 1 cm/½ in wide. Secure over the orange icing around the cake. Cut another strip, 5 mm/¼ in wide, and use to complete the border.

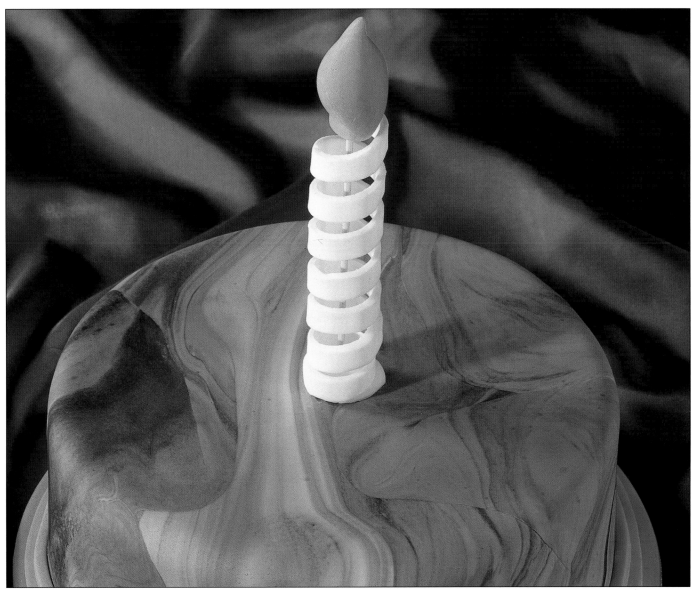

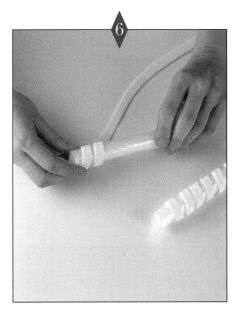

6 Wrap the candles in cling film (plastic wrap), twisting ends together. (One candle is prepared as a spare.) Roll the reserved white sugarpaste (fondant) to a long thin strip cut vertically into two sections, each about 5 mm/¼ in wide. Starting from one end of a covered candle, coil the icing around the candle, trimming off any excess icing at end. Leave for at least 48 hours to harden.

7 To release the icing, untwist the cling film (plastic wrap) and gently push out the candle inside. Carefully peel away the cling film (plastic wrap).

8 Place a dot of white icing in the centre of the cake and use to secure the icing candle. Push the bamboo skewer down through the centre to finish.

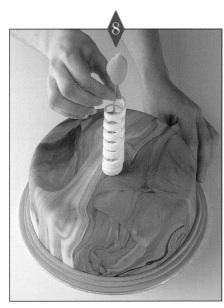

INDIAN ELEPHANT

This is a cake to say happy birthday to children and adults alike. Be as colourful as you like when decorating the elephant – dress it up for a very special occasion.

INGREDIENTS

Serves 30
- *30 cm/12 in square Madeira cake*
- *675 g/1½ lb/1½ lb butter icing*
- *225 g/8 oz/1½ lb marzipan*
- *black, holly green, mint green, yellow, mulberry food colourings*
- *chocolate coins, silver balls, coloured chocolate buttons, white chocolate buttons, liquorice allsorts (candy), Smartie (M&M)*
- *125 g/4 oz/¼ lb desiccated (dry unsweetened shredded) coconut*
- *30 ml/2 tbsp/2 tbsp apricot glaze*

MATERIALS AND EQUIPMENT

- *stiff paper for template*
- *36 cm/14 in square cakeboard*
- *cocktail stick (or toothpick)*

STORING

Kept in an airtight container, the cake will stay fresh for up to three days.

FREEZING

Not recommended.

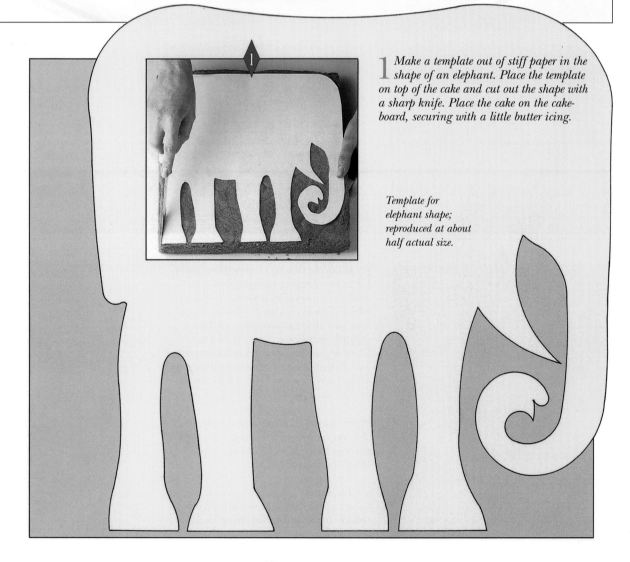

1 Make a template out of stiff paper in the shape of an elephant. Place the template on top of the cake and cut out the shape with a sharp knife. Place the cake on the cakeboard, securing with a little butter icing.

Template for elephant shape; reproduced at about half actual size.

2 *Colour the remaining butter icing pale grey, using the black food colour. Cover the top and sides of the cake with the icing carefully, so as not to loosen the cake crumbs. Swirl with a palette knife (spatula).*

3 *Using a cocktail stick dipped in black food colour, swirl in black highlights.*

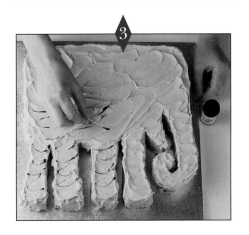

4 *Taking half of the marzipan, roll out and cut out shapes for the elephant's tusk, headpiece and blanket. Place them in position on the cake. Colour the remaining marzipan pink, yellow and holly green. Roll out and cut out patterns for the blanket, headpiece, trunk and tail. Roll small balls of yellow and pink to make the ankle bracelets.*

5 *Place all in position to decorate the elephant, along with the coins, silver balls, chocolate buttons (using the white ones, halved for the toe nails) and a liquorice allsort and Smartie (M&M) for the eye.*

6 *Rub a little mint green food colour into the coconut with your fingers until well mixed, to represent grass. Brush any uncovered cakeboard with a little apricot glaze and sprinkle the coconut over, in and around the elephant, carefully so as not to touch the icing.*

CHRISTMAS CRACKER

A festive cake that is fun to make and fun to eat. To make sure it is really fresh for your Christmas party, the cake can be made and decorated a day or two ahead of time, then simply cut it in half and arrange on the cakeboard with the colourful decorations to serve.

INGREDIENTS

Serves 8
- 4-egg quantity whisked sponge cake
- 225 g/8 oz/½ lb jam, for filling
- 30 ml/2 tbsp/2 tbsp apricot glaze
- 625 g/1 lb 6 oz/1 lb 6 oz sugarpaste (fondant) icing
- Christmas red, mint green, yellow, black, blue food colouring
- red, gold and green foil-wrapped chocolate eggs, coins and bars

MATERIALS AND EQUIPMENT

- 33 × 23 cm/13 × 9 in Swiss (jelly) roll tin (pan)
- 2 small red candles
- 32–36 cm/13–14 in cakeboard

STORING

Kept in an airtight container, the cake will stay fresh for up to three days.

FREEZING

Not recommended.

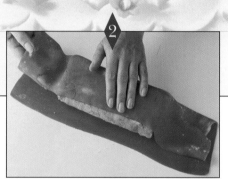

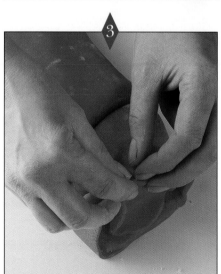

1 Preheat the oven to 180°C/350°F/Gas 4. Grease and line a 33 × 23 cm/13 × 9 in Swiss (jelly) roll tin (pan). Spoon the cake mixture into the prepared tin (pan) and bake in the preheated oven for 20–25 minutes. Allow to cool, spread with the jam and make into a roll. Cut 2.5 cm/1 in off each end of the Swiss (jelly) roll. Cut each piece in half. Set aside. Brush the outside of the roll with the apricot glaze.

2 Take 450 g/1 lb sugarpaste (fondant) and colour it red. Roll it out so it is 15 cm/6 in longer than the length of the trimmed cake, and wide enough to wrap around it. Position the cake in the centre of the red sugarpaste (fondant) icing and wrap around to cover, keeping the join underneath. Secure with water and trim where necessary.

3 Pinch the icing slightly where it meets the ends of the cake to resemble a cracker, and place the reserved pieces of cake inside each end of the icing to support them. Using any red icing trimmings, cut out two circles the same diameter as the ends of the cracker. Dampen the edges and position one at each end of the cracker, pressing together to seal.

4 Use the remaining icing as follows: colour most of it green and yellow for the decorations, leave a little white for the snowman, and colour a very small amount black and blue. Roll out the green and yellow icing. Cut strips with a knife and small circles with a small cutter or end of a large piping nozzle to decorate the cracker. Arrange the decorations on the cracker, securing with a little water.

5 Make the snowman with the white icing. Shape the body, head, arms and legs separately, then attach to the body, securing with a little water. Shape the hat, eyes and mouth from the black icing, the, bow tie from the green, buttons from the red, and a nose from the blue. Position these on the snowman, securing with a little water. Press two small red candles into his arms to hold. Leave to set.

6 When ready to serve, cut the cake in half, making jagged edges, and position on the cakeboard. Sit the snowman on top of one half and arrange the wrapped sweets around the board.

TERRACOTTA FLOWERPOT

A cake ideal for celebrating a gardener's birthday, Mother's Day or a Happy Retirement. The cake is baked in a pudding basin (deep bowl) for the flowerpot shape and filled with a colourful arrangement of icing flowers and foliage.

INGREDIENTS

Serves 15
- 3-egg quantity Madeira cake mixture
- 175 g/6 oz/6 oz jam
- 175 g/6 oz/6 oz butter icing
- 30 ml/2 tbsp/2 tbsp apricot glaze
- 575 g/1¼ lb/1¼ lb sugarpaste (fondant) icing
- 125 g/4 oz/⅓ cup royal icing, for fixing
- dark orange-red, black, red, silver, green, purple, yellow food colouring
- 2 chocolate-flake bars, coarsely crushed

MATERIALS AND EQUIPMENT

- 1.1 l/2 pt/5 cup pudding basin (deep bowl)
- greaseproof (wax) paper
- string
- fine paintbrush
- thin green wire
- 23 cm/9 in round cakeboard

STORING

Kept in an airtight container, the cake will stay fresh for up to three days.

FREEZING

Not recommended.

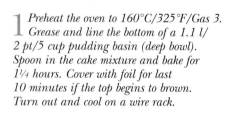

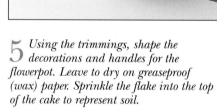

1 Preheat the oven to 160°C/325°F/Gas 3. Grease and line the bottom of a 1.1 l/2 pt/5 cup pudding basin (deep bowl). Spoon in the cake mixture and bake for 1¼ hours. Cover with foil for last 10 minutes if the top begins to brown. Turn out and cool on a wire rack.

2 When cold trim the top of the cake flat if it has domed. Cut the cake horizontally into three, and fill with the jam and butter icing.

3 Cut out a shallow circle from the top of the cake, leaving a 1 cm/½ in rim round the edge.

4 Brush the outside of the cake and the rim with the apricot glaze. Take 400 g/14 oz/scant 1 lb of the sugarpaste (fondant) icing and colour deep orange-red. Measure round the cake at its widest part and its height, with string. Roll out the deep orange-red-coloured icing to this measurement, remembering to add the width of the rim to the height. Wrap the icing round the cake and over the rim, moulding gently with your hands to fit. Reserve the trimmings, wrapped. Leave the cake to dry for several hours.

5 Using the trimmings, shape the decorations and handles for the flowerpot. Leave to dry on greaseproof (wax) paper. Sprinkle the flake into the top of the cake to represent soil.

6 Colour a small piece of the remaining sugarpaste (fondant) icing a very pale orange-red, roll out into an oblong and fold over to form a seed bag. Leave to dry then paint on a pattern with a fine paintbrush. Colour a very small piece of icing black and make the seeds. Leave to dry on greaseproof (wax) paper. Colour two more small pieces of icing red and silver and shape the trowel, leaving it to dry over a wooden spoon handle. Colour the remaining icing green, purple and a very small amount yellow.

8 *Shape the leaves and short stems with the green icing using your fingers and mark the veins with the back of a knife. Insert short pieces of thin green wire up some of the stems, so you can create different heights when they go into the flowerpot. Leave to dry over the handle of a wooden spoon. Roll out any remaining green icing and cut to represent grass.*

7 *Shape the flowers with the purple icing by moulding the petals individually and attaching together with royal icing. Roll out the yellow icing and cut out the flower centres with a small knife. Position in the middle of each flower with a small ball of yellow icing, securing with royal icing. Leave to dry on greaseproof (wax) paper.*

9 *Attach the deep orange-red decorations on the flowerpot with royal icing. Arrange the leaves and flowers in the pot. Place on the cakeboard and place the trowel, seed packet and grass around the outside.*

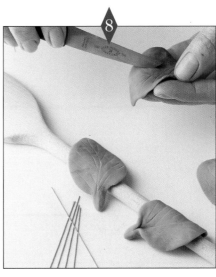

GLITTERING STAR

With a quick flick of a paintbrush you can give a sparkling effect to this glittering cake. Add some shimmering stars and moons and you have a cake ready to celebrate a birthday, Christmas, Halloween or silver wedding anniversary – all for the stars in your life.

INGREDIENTS

Serves 20–25

- 20 cm/8 in round rich fruit cake
- 40 ml/2½ tbsp/2½ tbsp apricot glaze
- 675 g/1½ lb/1½ lb marzipan
- 450 g/1 lb/1 lb sugarpaste (fondant) icing
- 125 g/4 oz/⅓ cup royal icing for fixing
- silver, gold, lilac shimmer, red sparkle, glitter green, primrose sparkle food colourings

MATERIALS AND EQUIPMENT

- greaseproof (wax) paper
- paintbrush
- stiff paper for templates
- 25 cm/10 in round cakeboard or plate

STORING

Kept in an airtight container, the cake will keep for up to three weeks.

FREEZING

Not recommended.

Moons and stars templates; reproduced at about half actual size.

1 Brush the cake with the apricot glaze. Roll out two-thirds of the marzipan and cover the cake. Leave to dry for 12 hours.

2 Roll out the sugarpaste (fondant) icing. Brush the marzipanned cake with a little water to slightly dampen and cover the cake with the sugarpaste (fondant) icing. Leave to dry for several hours.

3 Place the cake on a large sheet of greaseproof (wax) paper. Water down a little powdered silver food colouring and, using a paintbrush loaded with the colour, flick this all over the cake to give a spattered effect. Allow to dry.

4 Make templates out of stiff paper in two or three different-sized moon shapes and three or four irregular star shapes. Take the remaining marzipan, divide into five pieces and colour silver, gold, lilac, pink, green and yellow. Roll out each colour and cut into stars and moons using the templates as a guide, cutting some of the stars in half.

5 Place the cut-out shapes on the greaseproof (wax) paper, brush each with its own colour in powdered form to add more glitter. Allow to dry for several hours.

6 Position the cake on the cakeboard, securing underneath with a dab of royal icing, or place on a plate. Arrange the stars and moons at different angles all over the cake, attaching with royal icing, and position the halved stars upright as though coming out of the cake. Allow to set.

PORCUPINE

Melt-in-the-mouth strips of flaky chocolate bars give this porcupine its spiky coating, and a quick-mix moist chocolate cake makes the base. It's a fun cake for a children's or adults' party.

INGREDIENTS

Serves 15

- 3-egg quantity chocolate-flavoured quick-mix sponge cake
- 575 g/1¼ lb/1¼ lb chocolate-flavoured butter icing
- 50 g/2 oz/2 oz white marzipan
- cream, black, green, red, brown food colourings
- 5–6 chocolate flake bars

MATERIALS AND EQUIPMENT

- greaseproof (wax) paper
- 1.1 l/2 pt/5 cup pudding basin (deep bowl)
- 600 ml/1 pt/2½ cup pudding basin (deep bowl)
- 36 cm/14 in long rectangular cakeboard
- cocktail stick (or toothpick)
- fine paintbrush

STORING

Kept in a container in the refrigerator, the cake will stay fresh for up to three days.

FREEZING

Not recommended.

1 Preheat the oven to 160°C/325°F/Gas 3. Grease and line the bottoms of a 1.1 l/2 pt/5 cup and a 600 ml/1 pt/2½ cup pudding basin (deep bowl). Spoon the cake mixture into both basins (bowls) to two-thirds full. Bake in the preheated oven, allowing 55 mins–1 hr for the larger basin (bowl) and 35–40 mins for the smaller basin (bowl). Turn out and allow to cool on a wire rack.

2 Place both cakes on a surface so the widest ends are underneath. Take the smaller cake and, holding a sharp knife at an angle, slice off a piece from either side to create a pointed nose at one end.

3 Place the larger cake on the cakeboard behind the smaller one. Cut one of the cut-off slices in half and position either side, between the larger and small cake, to fill in the side gaps. Place the other cut-off piece on top to fill in the top gap, securing all with a little butter icing.

4 Spread the remaining butter icing all over the cake. On the pointed face part, make markings with a cocktail stick.

5 Break or cut the flake bars into thin strips and stick into the butter icing over the body of the porcupine to represent spikes.

6 Reserve a small portion of marzipan. Divide the remainder into three and colour one portion black, one green and one cream. Colour a tiny portion of the reserved, white marzipan brown for the apple stems. With the cream marzipan shape the ears and feet, using black and white make the eyes, and with the rest of the black shape the nose and the claws for the feet. With the green marzipan make the apples, painting on red markings with a fine paintbrush. Position the stems. Place everything except the apples in its proper place on the porcupine cake. Finally, place the apples on the board by the front of the porcupine.

TROPICAL PARROT

Create a tropical feel to any celebration with this colourful, exotic cake, whether for a Bon Voyage to faraway places or a simple birthday. The cake is made from one round Madeira cake, cutting out three easy shapes to give the parrot's body, tail and the branch it sits on. You can then be as decorative as you like with the markings and foliage.

INGREDIENTS

Serves 15
- 20 cm/8 in round Madeira cake
- 500 g/1 lb 2 oz/1 lb 2 oz butter icing
- 450 g/1 lb/1 lb sugarpaste (fondant) icing
- red, brown, green, yellow, orange, blue, purple, pink, black food colouring

MATERIALS AND EQUIPMENT

- 20 cm/8 in round cake tin (pan)
- greaseproof (wax) paper
- stiff paper for templates
- 36 cm/14 in square cakeboard

STORING

Kept in an airtight container, the cake will stay fresh for up to three days.

FREEZING

Not recommended.

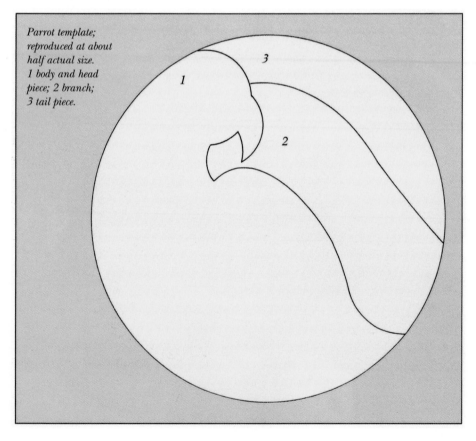

1 *Make templates out of stiff paper for the parrot's body, tail and branch. Place the templates on top of the cake and cut out the shapes with a sharp knife.*

2 *Take the sugarpaste (fondant) icing and colour about one-third red. Colour a quarter of the remaining piece brown and the rest yellow, pink, orange, blue, purple, black, green and light green. Leave a small amount white.*

Parrot template; reproduced at about half actual size. 1 body and head piece; 2 branch; 3 tail piece.

3 *Slice each piece of cake (body, tail and branch) in half horizontally and fill with some of the butter icing. Use the remaining butter icing to coat the outsides of the cake. Measure the length and depth of the cake that forms the branch. Roll out the brown icing in one piece large enough to cover it. Position over the cake branch and trim to fit.*

4 *Measure the length and depth of the sides of the parrot's body. Roll out some of the red icing and cut strips to match the measurements. Press onto the butter icing to fix in position. Roll out a piece of red icing for the top of the body, using the template as a guide. Leave out the face, beak and blue body parts. Position the red sugarpaste (fondant) on the butter icing, reserving the trimmings. Roll out a piece of white and some black icing for the face and beak, cut to fit and ease into position with your fingers. Do the same with a piece of blue icing to finish off the body, and with the tailpiece, using the rest of the reserved red icing.*

5 *Roll out the other coloured pieces of icing. Cut out pieces in the shape of feathers, some with jagged edges. Press these into position on the body and tail, easing to fit with your fingers. Secure with a little water, bending and twisting some of the 'feathers' to create different angles and heights. Cut out leaf and flower shapes for the branch out of the green and pink icings. Use templates as a guide, if wished.*

6 *Place the iced parrot pieces in position on the cakeboard. Make the eye for the parrot. Secure the eye onto the head with water, and use water to fix leaves and flower on the branch. If wished, colour an additional 125 g/4 oz/¼ lb sugarpaste (fondant) icing green. Roll and cut out more leaves to decorate the base of the parrot.*

HALLOWEEN PUMPKIN

Halloween is a time for spooky cakes – witches may even burst out of them. This one is made in two pudding basins (deep bowls), making it easy to create a pumpkin effect. Make the cake and icing with your favourite flavour – and you are all set for a party full of eerie surprises.

INGREDIENTS

Serves 15
- 3-egg quantity orange-flavoured Madeira cake mixture
- 250 g/9 oz/9 oz orange-flavoured butter icing
- 450 g/1 lb/1 lb sugarpaste (fondant) icing
- 125 g/4 oz/¼ lb royal icing for fixing
- orange, black, yellow food colourings

MATERIALS AND EQUIPMENT

- greaseproof (wax) paper
- 2 × 1.1 l/2 pt/5 cup pudding basins (deep bowls)
- thin wooden skewer
- thin paintbrush
- 23 cm/9 in round cakeboard

STORING

Kept in an airtight container, the cake will stay fresh for up to three days.

FREEZING

Not recommended.

1 Preheat the oven to 160°C/325°F/Gas3. Grease and line the bottoms of two 1.1 l/2 pt/5 cup pudding basins (deep bowls). Divide the cake mixture equally between them and bake for 1¼ hours. Turn out and cool on a wire rack.

2 Trim the widest ends of each cake so they will fit flat against one another to make a round shape. Split each cake in half horizontally and fill with some of the butter icing, then stick the two cakes together with butter icing to form a pumpkin. Trim one of the narrow ends off slightly, to give a better shape. Let this end be the bottom of the pumpkin. Cover the outside of the cake with the remaining butter icing.

3 Take 350 g/12 oz/¾ lb of the sugarpaste (fondant) icing and colour it orange. Roll out to cover the cake, trimming to fit where necessary. Mould it gently with your hands to give a smooth surface. Reserve the trimmings.

4 With a thin wooden skewer, mark the segments onto the pumpkin. With a fine paintbrush and watered-down orange food colouring, paint on the markings for the pumpkin flesh. Use orange sugarpaste (fondant) trimmings for the top of the cake where the witch bursts out, by cutting and tearing rolled out pieces to create jagged edges. Attach to the top of the cake with a little water.

5 Take the remaining sugarpaste (fondant) icing and colour three-quarters black. Of the remainder, colour a little yellow and leave the rest white. Use some of the black and white to make the witch, moulding the head, arms and body separately and securing with royal icing. When set, roll out some black icing and cut jagged edges to form a cape. Drape over the arms and body, securing with a little water. Make the hat in two pieces – a circle and a cone – and secure with royal icing. Leave to dry on greaseproof (wax) paper. Shape the cauldron, broomstick and cat's head out of more of the black and yellow icing, securing the handle of the cauldron with royal icing when dry. Leave all to dry completely on greaseproof (wax) paper.

6 Use the remaining black icing for the pumpkin features. Roll out and cut out the eyes, nose and mouth with a sharp knife. Attach to the pumpkin with a little water. Place the cake on the cakeboard, secure the witch on top of the cake with royal icing and arrange the cat, cauldron and broomstick around the base.

CHRISTENING SAMPLER

Instead of embroidering a sampler to welcome a newly-born baby, why not make a sampler cake to celebrate?

INGREDIENTS

Serves 30
- 20 cm/8 in square rich fruit cake
- 45 ml/3 tbsp/3 tbsp apricot glaze
- 450 g/1 lb/1 lb marzipan
- 675 g/1½ lb/1½ lb sugarpaste (fondant) icing
- brown, blue, pink, yellow, orange, green, cream, purple food colourings

MATERIALS AND EQUIPMENT

- 25 cm/10 in square cakeboard
- fine paintbrush
- small heart-shaped biscuit (cookie) cutter

STORING

Kept in an airtight container, the cake will stay fresh for up to three weeks.

FREEZING

Not recommended.

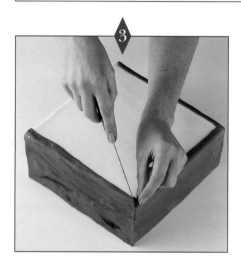

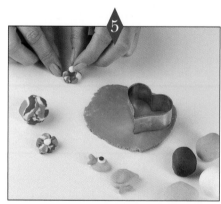

1 Brush the cake with apricot glaze. Roll out the marzipan, cover the cake and leave to dry for 12 hours.

2 Cut 450 g/1 lb/1 lb of the sugarpaste (fondant) icing into three. Take one-third and roll out to the size of the top of the cake. Brush the top of the cake with a little water and cover with the icing.

3 Take the other two-thirds of the icing for the sides and colour brown. Roll out in four separate pieces to the measured length and about 1 cm/½ in wider than the width of each side. Brush each side with a little water, then press each piece of brown icing on, folding over the extra width at the top to represent the edges of a picture frame. Cut off each corner at an angle to represent the mitred join of the frame. Reserve any brown trimmings. Place the cake on the cakeboard.

4 With a fine paintbrush, paint over the sides with watered-down brown food colouring to represent wood grain.

5 Take the remaining sugarpaste (fondant) icing and colour small amounts yellow, orange, brown, purple, cream, two shades of blue, green and pink. Leave a little white. Use these colours to shape the ducks, teddy bear, bulrushes, water, apple-blossom branch and leaves. Roll out a small piece of pink icing and cut out a heart with a small heart-shaped biscuit (cookie) cutter (or use a template). Roll out a small piece of white icing and cut out the baby's initial with a small sharp knife.

For the border, roll out strips of blue and yellow icing and cut into oblongs and squares; make small balls and small squares out of the purple icing. For the apple blossom, gently work together the pale pink, deep pink and white sugarpaste (fondant) to give a marbled effect. Shape the flowers from this, placing a small white ball in the centre. Attach all the decorations onto the cake with a little water as you make them.

6 With any leftover colours, roll out long strips of icing with your hands to make 'threads'. Form them into loops, attaching the joins with water. Use small strips of brown icing trimmings to hold the threads together. Arrange around the base of the cake on the board.

MARKET STALL

An open-air market stall is the theme for this cake, bursting with colourful produce. Vary this design if you wish, adding as wide a variety of fruit and vegetables as you wish.

INGREDIENTS

Serves 30

- 20 cm/8 in square rich fruit cake
- 45 ml/3 tbsp/3 tbsp apricot glaze
- 900 g/2 lb/2 lb marzipan
- 450 g/1 lb/1 lb sugarpaste (fondant) icing
- 125 g/4 oz/¼ lb royal icing, for fixing
- brown, green, red, orange, yellow, peach, purple, pink, black food colourings

MATERIALS AND EQUIPMENT

- greaseproof (wax) paper
- 25 cm/10 in square cakeboard
- fine paintbrush

STORING

Kept in an airtight container, the cake will stay fresh for up to three weeks.

FREEZING

Not recommended.

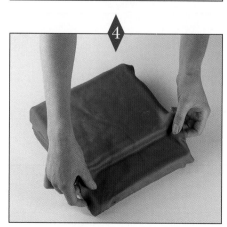

1 Slice 4 cm/1½ in off one side of the cake. Brush the cake with apricot glaze. Take half of the marzipan (reserve the other half for shaping the fruits and vegetables). Roll out three-quarters of it and cover the large piece of cake with it. With the other quarter of marzipan, cover one long side, the top and the two short sides of the cake slice. Leave to dry for 12 hours.

2 Colour half of the sugarpaste (fondant) icing brown and the other half green. Using three-quarters of the brown icing, cover three sides of the large cake (not the cut side), brushing the marzipan first with a little water to secure the icing. With the other quarter of brown icing, cover the marzipanned sides of the smaller piece of cake, measuring first to fit and brushing the marzipan with a little water to stick. Reserve any brown icing trimmings. With these trimmings, roll out and cut narrow dividers to fit the top of the cake. Leave the dividers on greaseproof (wax) paper to dry for several hours.

3 Place the large piece of cake on the cakeboard, with the smaller one in front to create a different level. Attach the cakes together with royal icing and use icing to attach to the board.

4 Measure the length and width of the cake, including the lower level. Roll out the green icing about 4 cm/1½ in wider and longer than the measured length and width. Brush the marzipan on the tops of the cakes with a little water and cover the cakes with the green icing. Allow it to fall naturally in folds over the edges. Leave the cake to dry for several hours.

5 Take the remaining 450 g/1 lb/1 lb marzipan, reserve a little for the stall holder and colour the rest red, orange, yellow, green, brown, peach and purple. Use these colours to shape the fruits and vegetables. Add markings with a fine paintbrush onto the melons, peaches and potatoes. For the front of the stall, shape baskets and a potato sack out of different shades of brown. For the stallholder, colour the reserved marzipan pink, purple, black and flesh-coloured and shape the head, body and arms separately, attaching with a little royal icing. Make the hands and face features and the hair, and press on with a little water. Place a melon in her arms to hold. Leave all to dry on greaseproof (wax) paper for several hours.

6 *Attach the dividers, the baskets and the stallholder onto the cake with royal icing. Arrange the produce in piles on the stall between the dividers and in the baskets, and the sack of potatoes in the front.*

RACING RING

A simple ring cake makes the perfect base for this teddy-bear racing track. Choose the flattest and widest end of the cake for the top (this will depend on the shape of your ring mould), so there's plenty of room for the icing cars to race around on.

INGREDIENTS

Serves 12

- 2-egg quantity quick-mix sponge cake mixture
- 350 g/12 oz/¾ lb butter icing
- 500 g/1 lb 2 oz/1 lb 2 oz sugarpaste (fondant) icing
- 125 g/4 oz/¼ lb royal icing, for fixing
- black, blue, yellow, green, orange, red, purple food colourings
- selection of miniature liquorice sweets (candies), dolly mixtures and teddy bears
- 113 g/4½ oz packet liquorice Catherine wheels

MATERIALS AND EQUIPMENT

- 22 cm/8½ in ring mould
- 25 cm/10 in round cakeboard
- 1 thin wooden kebab skewer
- fine paintbrush
- greaseproof (wax) paper

STORING

Kept in an airtight container, the cake will stay fresh for up to three days.

FREEZING

Not recommended.

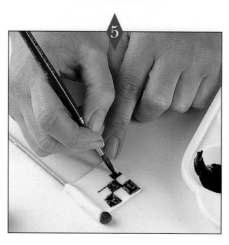

1 Preheat the oven to 160°C/325°F/Gas 3. Spoon the cake mixture into a greased ring mould. Bake for 35–40 minutes. Turn out and cool on a wire rack.

2 Cut the cake in half horizontally and fill with some of the butter icing. Cover the outside of the cake with the remaining butter icing, having the widest part of the cake on top.

3 Cut 350 g/12 oz/¾ lb of the sugarpaste (fondant) icing in half. Use half for coating the top and inside ring of the cake and half for coating the outside. To coat the inside of the ring, cut one half of the icing in half again and roll out to the measured diameter and width, (reserve the other piece for the top). Press in position over the butter icing. Roll out the reserved piece for the top to the measured diameter and width (you may find this easier to do in two halves), pressing in position and easing into shape over the butter icing.

4 Take the half piece of icing reserved for coating the outside and roll out to the measured width and diameter. Press in position round the outside of the cake, reserving the white icing trimmings to make the flag. Place the cake on the cakeboard.

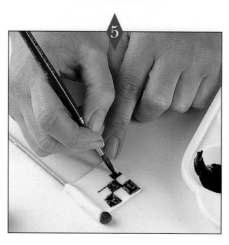

5 Take the reserved white icing trimmings and roll out to an oblong for the flag. Cut the wooden kebab skewer to a height of about 12.5 cm/5 in and fold one end of the flag round it, securing with a little water. With black food colouring and a fine paintbrush paint on a chequered pattern. Colour a small piece of icing black, make into a ball and stick on top of the skewer. Create a few folds in the flag and leave to dry on greaseproof (wax) paper.

6 Colour the remaining sugarpaste (fondant) icing blue, yellow, green, orange, red and a very small amount purple. Shape each car in two pieces, attaching in the centre with royal icing where the seat joins the body of the car. Add decorations and headlights and attach dolly mixture wheels with royal icing. Place a candy teddy bear in each car and leave to set.

7 Take the liquorice Catherine wheels and unwind them, removing the centre sweets. Lay the liquorice over the top of the cake to represent the track, leaving a gap in the middle and securing onto the cake with royal icing. Secure one strip round the bottom of the cake also.

8 Cut some of the liquorice into small strips and attach round the middle of the outside of the cake with royal icing. Arrange small liquorice sweets around the bottom of the cake. Position the cars on top of the cake on the tracks and attach the flag to the outside with royal icing.

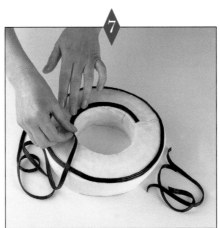

CHOCOLATE FRUIT BIRTHDAY CAKE

A moist chocolate Madeira cake is covered in marzipan and chocolate fudge icing. The fruits are moulded from coloured marzipan and make an eye-catching decoration.

INGREDIENTS

Serves 30
- 18 cm/7 in square deep chocolate-flavoured Madeira cake
- 45 ml/3 tbsp/3 tbsp apricot glaze
- 450 g/1 lb/1 lb homemade or commercial white marzipan
- 450 g/1 lb/1 lb chocolate fudge icing
- red, yellow, orange, green and purple food colouring

DECORATION

- selection of marzipan fruits
- whole cloves
- angelica strips
- 0.75 m/¾ yd × 1 cm/½ in wide yellow ribbon

MATERIALS AND EQUIPMENT

- greaseproof (wax) paper
- 18 cm/7 in square deep cake tin (pan)
- 20 cm/8 in square silver cakeboard
- wire rack
- nylon piping bag
- medium-sized gateau nozzle

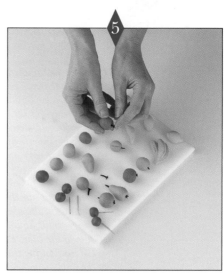

1 Bake the cake and allow to cool on a wire rack. Cut a slice off the top of the cake to level if necessary and invert on to the cakeboard. Brush evenly with apricot glaze.

2 Roll out two-thirds of the marzipan thinly to a 25 cm/10 in square. Place over the cake and smooth the top and down the sides. Trim off the excess marzipan around the base of the cake. Knead the trimmings together and reserve for making the marzipan fruits.

3 Place the cake on a wire rack over a tray and pour the freshly-made chocolate fudge icing over the cake, spreading quickly with a palette knife (metal spatula). Allow the excess icing to fall on the tray. Leave for 10 minutes, then place on to the cakeboard.

4 Using the remaining icing, place in a nylon piping bag fitted with a medium-sized gateau nozzle. Pipe a row of stars around the top edge and base of the cake. Leave to set.

5 Using the reserved marzipan, food colouring, cloves and angelica strips, model a selection of fruits.

6 Measure and fit the ribbon around the side of the cake and secure with a pin. Decorate the top with marzipan fruits.

EIGHTEENTH BIRTHDAY CAKE

A really striking cake for a lucky someone celeb-rating their eighteenth birthday. Change the shape if you cannot hire the tin (pan).

INGREDIENTS

Serves 80

- 33.5 × 20 cm/13½ × 8 in diamond-shaped deep rich or light fruit cake (make using quantities for a standard 23 cm/9 in round cake)
- 45 ml/3 tbsp/3 tbsp apricot glaze
- 1.1 kg/2½ lb/2½ lb homemade or commercial white marzipan
- 1.6 kg/3½ lb/3½ lbs white sugarpaste (fondant)
- black food colouring
- 30 ml/2 tbsp/2 tbsp royal icing

DECORATION

- 2 m/2 yd × 2.5 cm/1 in wide white ribbon
- ½ m/½ yd × 2 mm/⅛ in wide black ribbon

MATERIALS AND EQUIPMENT

- '18' numeral cutter or template
- greaseproof (wax) paper piping bag
- No. 1 plain writing nozzle

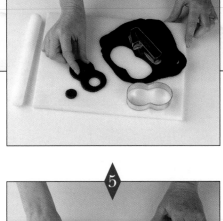

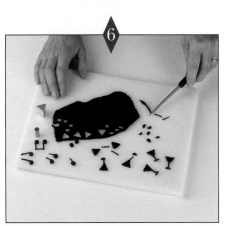

1 Bake the cake and allow to cool. Brush with apricot glaze and place on the cakeboard. Cover with marzipan.

2 Cover the cake using 1.1 kg/2½ lb/ 2½ lb sugarpaste (fondant). Knead the trimmings into the remaining sugarpaste (fondant) and colour using black food colouring.

3 Roll out two-thirds of the black sugarpaste (fondant) and cut into four strips the width and length of each section of the cakeboard. Brush the board with apricot glaze and place each strip in position; trim to fit neatly.

4 Roll-out one-quarter of the remaining sugarpaste (fondant) and cut out the number '18' using a special biscuit (cookie) cutter or by cutting round a template. Leave on a piece of foam sponge to dry.

5 Roll out some more icing thinly and cut out 40 triangles for the bow ties and 20 for the wine glasses.

6 Use a tiny round cutter or the end of a plain nozzle to cut out 20 music notes and 10 bases for the glasses, cut in half. Cut out thin strips of icing for the tails of the music notes and the stems of the glasses.

7 Using a greaseproof (wax) paper piping bag fitted with a No. 1 plain writing nozzle, half-fill with royal icing coloured black. Join the bow ties together with tiny beads of icing. Attach the music notes to their tails and the glasses to the stems and bases. Leave them all to dry.

8 Arrange the '18', music notes, wine glasses and bow ties over the top of the cake and attach each with a bead of icing. Continue to fix the decorations onto the sides of the cake.

CHRISTMAS STOCKING CAKE

A bright and happy cake to make for Christmas. Make the stocking and parcels in advance to save time at Christmas.

<table>
<tr><td>INGREDIENTS</td><td>DECORATION</td><td>MATERIALS AND EQUIPMENT</td></tr>
</table>

INGREDIENTS

Serves 50
- 20 cm/8 in square rich fruit cake
- 45 ml/3 tbsp/3 tbsp apricot glaze
- 900 g/2 lb/2 lb homemade or commercial white marzipan
- 1.1 kg/2½ lb/2 ½ lb sugarpaste (fondant) icing
- 15 ml/1 tbsp/1 tbsp royal icing
- red and green food colouring

DECORATION
- 1¼ m/1¼ yd × 2 cm/¾ in wide red ribbon
- 1 m/1 yd × 2 cm/¾ in wide green ribbon

MATERIALS AND EQUIPMENT
- 25 cm/10 in square silver cakeboard
- card for template

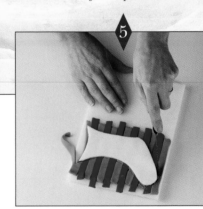

1 Bake the cake and allow to cool. Brush with apricot glaze and place on the cakeboard. Cover the cake with marzipan.

2 Reserve 225 g/8 oz/½ lb sugarpaste (fondant) icing for decorations, and use the remainder to cover the cake smoothly. Place the cake in a box and leave to dry in a warm dry place. Measure and fit the red ribbon around the board, securing with a pin, and the green ribbon around the cake, securing with royal icing.

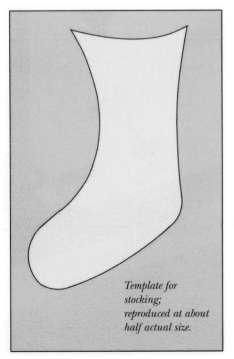

Template for stocking; reproduced at about half actual size.

3 Knead the sugarpaste (fondant) trimmings together. Reserve 125 g/4 oz/¼ lb and cut the remainder in half; colour one half red and the other half green with food colouring. Trace the template of the stocking onto card and cut out. Roll out a piece of white sugarpaste (fondant) and cut out round the template.

4 Roll out the red and green sugarpaste (fondant) to 5 mm/¼ in thick and cut each into seven 1 cm/½ in strips. Remove alternate green strips and replace with red strips. Gently roll the stripey sugarpaste (fondant) together.

5 Use the template to cut out another stocking shape, allowing an extra 5 mm/¼ in all around.

6 Brush the white stocking with apricot glaze and, using a palette knife (metal spatula), lift the striped stocking and place over the white one. Press lightly together and leave to dry.

7 Shape the remaining white sugarpaste (fondant) into four parcel shapes and trim each with thin strips of red and green sugarpaste (fondant) ribbons.

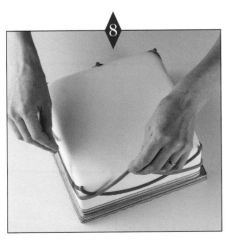

8 Knead the remaining green and red sugarpaste (fondant) together, keeping the colours separate. Roll out each into a 20 cm/8 in strip, 1 cm/½ in wide. Cut each into two 5 mm/¼ in strips. Pipe a bead of royal icing on to each corner, press alternate green and red strips in position and trim to size. Shape four red and four green balls and press in position where the sugarpaste (fondant) strips join, securing with a little royal icing.

9 Arrange the stocking and parcels in position on the top of the cake. Leave to dry.

KULICH

This Russian yeasted cake – Kulich – is known under other names in many Eastern European countries. Traditionally made at Easter time in Slavic countries, this delicious spiced cake was baked in special moulds. For convenience the recipe has been converted for use in either clay flower pots, or coffee tins (cans). Capacity and sizes have been given for both.

INGREDIENTS

Makes 2 cakes
- 15 ml/1 tbsp/1 tbsp dried yeast
- 90 ml/6 tbsp/6 tbsp tepid milk
- 75 g/3 oz/6 tbsp caster (superfine) sugar
- 500 g/1 lb 2 oz/4½ cups plain (all-purpose) flour
- pinch saffron strands
- 30 ml/2 tbsp/2 tbsp dark rum
- 2.5 ml/½ tsp/½ tsp ground cardamom
- 2.5 ml/½ tsp/½ tsp ground cumin
- 50 g/2 oz/¼ cup unsalted butter
- 2 eggs plus 2 egg yolks
- ½ vanilla pod, finely chopped
- 25 g/1 oz/2 tbsp each: chopped mixed candied peel, chopped crystallized ginger, chopped almonds and currants

DECORATION

- 75 g/3 oz/¼ cup icing (confectioners') sugar, sifted
- 7.5–10 ml/1½–2 tsp/1½–2 tsp warm water
- a drop almond essence (extract)
- 2 candles
- blanched almonds
- mixed candied peel

MATERIALS AND EQUIPMENT

- greaseproof (wax) paper
- 2 × 15 cm/6 in clay flower pots or 2 × 500 g/1 lb 2 oz/1⅛ lb coffee tins (cans)

FREEZING

Recommended before the cakes are iced. Wrap and freeze. Defrost and continue.

STORING

Best eaten the day of making.

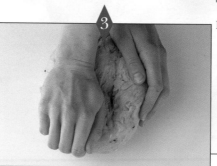

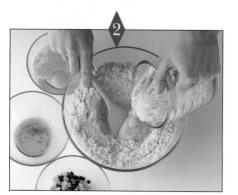

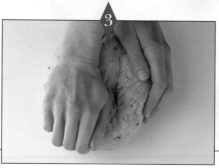

1 Blend the yeast, milk, 25 g/1 oz/2 tbsp sugar and 50 g/2 oz/½ cup flour together, until smooth. Leave in a warm place for 15 minutes, until frothy. Soak the saffron in the rum for 15 minutes.

2 Sift the remaining flour and spices into a bowl and rub in the butter. Stir in the remaining sugar, make a well in the centre and work in the frothed yeast mixture, the saffron liquid and remaining ingredients to form a fine dough.

3 Knead on a lightly floured surface for 5 minutes until smooth and pliable. Place in an oiled bowl, cover and leave to rise in a warm place for 1–1½ hours, until doubled in size.

4 Preheat oven to 190°C/375°F/Gas 5. Grease, base-line and flour the pots or tins (cans).

5 Knock back (punch down) the dough. Divide in two and form each lump into rounds. Press into the prepared pots, cover and leave in a warm place for a further 30 minutes, until the dough comes two-thirds of the way up the sides.

6 Bake for 35 minutes if using the coffee tins (cans) or 50 minutes if using the clay pots. Test with a skewer and remove from the oven. Transfer to a wire rack and leave to cool.

7 Blend the icing (confectioners') sugar, water and almond essence (extract) together until smooth, to form a thick glacé icing. Pour over the top of each cake, allowing it to drizzle down the sides, and decorate with the candles, nuts and peel.

ST CLEMENTS MARBLED CROWN

A tangy orange-and-lemon marbled cake is transformed into a spectacular centrepiece by the pretty arrangement of fresh flowers in the centre of the ring. The icing is decorated with crystallized fruits, dragées and sugared almonds, creating a dramatic jewelled effect.

INGREDIENTS

Serves 8
- 175 g/6 oz/¾ cup butter
- 75 g/3 oz/good ⅓ cup light soft brown sugar
- 3 eggs, separated
- grated rind and juice 1 orange
- 160 g/5½ oz/1⅓ cups self-raising flour
- 75 g/3 oz/6 tbsp caster (superfine) sugar
- grated rind and juice of 1 lemon
- 15 g/½ oz/2 tbsp ground almonds
- 350 ml/¾ pt/1 US pt double (heavy) cream
- 15 ml/1 tbsp/1 tbsp Grand Marnier

DECORATION
- 16 crystallized orange and lemon slices
- silver dragées
- 8 gold sugared almonds
- fresh flowers

MATERIALS AND EQUIPMENT
- 850 ml/1½ pt/3¾ cups capacity ring mould
- skewer

STORING

Best eaten the day of making.

FREEZING

Recommended at the end of step 5. Wrap and freeze. Defrost at room temperature and ice and decorate.

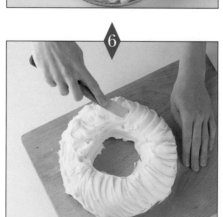

1 Preheat oven to 180°C/350°F/Gas 4. Grease and flour the mould.

2 Make orange cake mixture. Cream half the butter and the soft brown sugar together until pale and light. Gradually beat in the egg yolks, orange rind and juice until incorporated, and fold in 75 g/3 oz/¾ cup of the flour.

3 Make lemon cake mixture. Cream the remaining butter and caster (superfine) sugar together, stir in the lemon rind and juice and fold in the remaining flour and ground almonds. Whisk the egg whites until stiff, and fold in.

4 Spoon the two mixtures alternately into the prepared tin (pan).

5 Using a skewer or small spoon, swirl through the mixture, to create a marble effect. Bake for 45–50 minutes, until risen and a skewer, inserted into the cake, comes out clean. Cool in the tin (pan) for 10 minutes and transfer to a wire rack to cool completely.

6 Whip the cream and Grand Marnier together until lightly thickened. Spread over the cooled cake and swirl a pattern over the icing.

7 Decorate the ring with the crystallized fruits, dragées and almonds to resemble a jewelled crown. Arrange a few pretty, fresh flowers in the centre.

MOTHER'S DAY BASKET

Every mother would love to receive a cake like this on Mother's Day. Choose fresh flowers to decorate the top.

INGREDIENTS	DECORATION	MATERIALS AND EQUIPMENT
Serves 12 ● *3-egg quantity of orange-flavoured quick-mix sponge cake* ● *900 g/2 lb/2 lb orange-flavoured butter icing*	● *1 m/1 yd × 1 cm/½ in wide mauve ribbon* ● *½ m/½ yd × 2 mm/⅛ in wide spotted mauve ribbon* ● *fresh flowers*	● *1.1 l/2 pt/5 cup fluted ovenproof glass dish* ● *15 cm/6 in round silver cakecard* ● *greaseproof (wax) paper piping bags* ● *basket-weave nozzle* ● *kitchen foil*

1 *Lightly grease and line the base of a fluted ovenproof glass dish (or brioche mould). Make the cake without any baking powder and bake in the oven for 1 hour 15 minutes to 1 hour 25 minutes until well risen, golden brown and firm to the touch.*

2 *Spread the side of the cake with one-third of the orange-flavoured butter icing and place upside down on a board.*

3 *Make plenty of greaseproof (wax) paper piping bags and fit with a basket-weave nozzle. Half-fill with butter icing and pipe the sides with a basket-weave pattern (see Basket-weave Wedding Cake).*

4 *Invert the cake onto the cakecard and spread the top with butter icing. Pipe a shell edging, using the basket-weave nozzle, to neaten the top edge. Continue to pipe the basket-weave icing across the top of the cake, starting at the edge. Leave the cake to set in a cool place.*

5 *Fold a piece of foil in half, then half again and continue to fold until you have a strip several layers thick.*

6 *Using the ribbon, bind the strip to cover the foil; bend up the end to secure the ribbon. Bend the foil to make a handle, and press into the icing.*

7 *Choose some flowers and make a neat arrangement tied with ribbon on top of the cake just before serving. Tie a bow and pin it to the sides of the cake.*

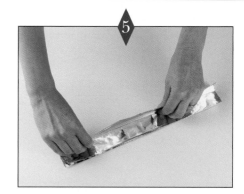

BASIC RECIPES AND TECHNIQUES

BASIC RECIPES & TECHNIQUES

A quick mix sponge cake is light and fluffy; ideal for this springtime cake decorated with lemon butter icing and marzipan flowers.

Quick Mix Sponge Cake

This is a quick-and-easy reliable recipe for making everyday cakes in various sizes, shapes and flavours.

INGREDIENTS	2-EGG QUANTITY	3-EGG QUANTITY	4-EGG QUANTITY
● Self-raising flour	125 g/4 oz/1 cup	175 g/6 oz/1½ cups	225 g/8 oz/2 cups
● Baking powder	5 ml/1 tsp/1 tsp	7.5 ml/1½ tsp/1½ tsp	10 ml/2 tsp/2 tsp
● Caster (superfine) sugar	125 g/4 oz/½ cup	175 g/6 oz/¾ cup	225 g/8 oz/1 cup
● Soft margarine	125 g/4 oz/½ cup	175 g/6 oz/¾ cup	225 g/8 oz/1 cup
● Eggs	2	3	4

1 *Preheat the oven to 170°C/325°F/ Gas 3. Prepare the tin (pan) according to the recipe.*

2 *Sift the flour and baking powder into a bowl. Add sugar, margarine and eggs. Mix together with a wooden spoon, then beat for 1–2 minutes until the mixture is smooth and glossy.*

3 *Stir in chosen flavourings and beat until evenly blended.*

4 *Pour into prepared tin (pan), level the top and bake as required.*

CHOICE OF FLAVOURINGS

The following amounts are for a 2-egg quantity cake. Increase the suggested flavourings to suit the quantity being made.

Citrus – 10 ml/2 tsp/2 tsp finely grated orange, lemon or lime rind
Chocolate – add 15 ml/1 tbsp/1 tbsp cocoa blended with 15 ml/1 tbsp/ 1 tbsp boiling water, or 25 g/1 oz/ scant ¼ cup chocolate dots, melted
Coffee – 10 ml/2 tsp/2 tsp coffee granules blended with 5 ml/1 tsp/ 1 tsp boiling water
Nuts – replace 25 g/1 oz/2 tbsp flour with finely ground nuts

Madeira Cake

A good, plain cake which can be made as an alternative to a light or rich fruit cake. It is firm and moist, can be flavoured to taste, and makes a good base for icing and decorating.

A madeira cake is traditionally used for decorative novelty cakes, as it provides a firm and lasting sponge base.

MADEIRA CAKE CHART

Cake Tin Sizes	15 cm/6 in Square	18 cm/7 in Square	20 cm/8 in Square	23 cm/9 in Square	25 cm/10 in Square	28 cm/11 in Square	30 cm/12 in Square
	18 cm/7 in Round	20 cm/8 in Round	23 cm/9 in Round	25 cm/10 in Round	28 cm/11 in Round	30 cm/12 in Round	33 cm/13 in Round
INGREDIENTS							
Plain (all-purpose) flour	225 g/ 8 oz/ 2 cups	350 g/ 12 oz/ 3 cups	450 g/ 1 lb/ 4 cups	500 g/ 1 lb 2 oz/ 4½ cups	575 g/ 1¼ lb/ 5 cups	675 g/ 1½ lb/ 6 cups	900 g/ 2 lb/ 8 cups
Baking powder	5 ml/ 1 tsp/ 1 tsp	7.5 ml/ 1½ tsp/ 1½ tsp	10 ml/ 2 tsp/ 2 tsp	12.5 ml/ 2½ tsp/ 2½ tsp	15 ml/ 3 tsp/ 3 tsp	17.5 ml/ 3½ tsp/ 3½ tsp	20 ml/ 4 tsp/ 4 tsp
Caster (superfine) sugar	175 g/ 6 oz/ ¾ cup	275 g/ 10 oz/ 1¼ cups	400 g/ 14 oz/ 1¾ cups	450 g/ 1 lb/ 2 cups	500 g/ 1 lb 2 oz/ 2¼ cups	625 g/ 1 lb 6 oz/ 2¾ cups	725 g/ 1 lb 10 oz/ 3¼ cups
Soft margarine	175 g/ 6 oz/ ¾ cup	275 g/ 10 oz/ 1¼ cups	400 g/ 14 oz/ 1¾ cups	450 g/ 1 lb/ 2 cups	500 g/ 1 lb 2 oz/ 2¼ cups	625 g/ 1 lb 6 oz/ 2¾ cups	725 g/ 1 lb 10 oz/ 3¼ cups
Size 3 eggs	3	5	7	8	10	12	13
Milk	30 ml/ 2 tbsp/ 2 tbsp	45 ml/ 3 tbsp/ 3 tbsp	55 ml/ 3½ tbsp/ 3½ tbsp	60 ml/ 4 tbsp/ 4 tbsp	70 ml/ 4½ tbsp/ 4½ tbsp	75 ml/ 5 tbsp/ 5 tbsp	85 ml/ 5½ tbsp/ 5½ tbsp
Approx. Cooking Time	1¼–1½ hours	1½–1¾ hours	1¾–2 hours	1¾–2 hours	2–2¼ hours	2¼–2½ hours	2½–¾ hours

1 *Preheat the oven to 170°C/325°F/Gas 3.
Grease and line a deep cake tin (pan)
(see Lining Cake Tins/Pans).*

2 *Sift flour and baking powder into a
mixing bowl. Add sugar, margarine,
eggs and milk. Mix together with a wooden
spoon, then beat for 1–2 minutes until
smooth and glossy. Alternatively, use an
electric mixer and beat for 1 minute only.*

3 *Add any flavourings desired and mix
until well blended.*

CHOICE OF FLAVOURINGS

The following amounts are for a
3-egg quantity cake. Increase the
suggested flavourings to suit the
quantities being made.
Cherry – 175 g/6 oz/1 scant cup
glacé cherries, halved
Citrus – replace milk with lemon,
orange or lime juice and 5 ml/1 tsp/
1 tsp of grated lemon, orange or
lime rind
Coconut – 50 g/2 oz/1 cup desiccated
(dry unsweetened shredded) coconut
Nuts – replace 125 g/4 oz/1 cup flour
with ground almonds, hazelnuts,
walnuts or pecan nuts

4 *Place the mixture into the prepared tin
(pan) and spread evenly. Give the tin
(pan) a sharp tap to remove any air pockets.
Make a depression in the centre of the
mixture to ensure a level surface.*

5 *Bake the cake in the centre of the oven.
Follow the chart cooking times,
according to the size of the cake. It is cooked
when the cake springs back when lightly
pressed in the centre.*

STORING

Leave the cake to cool in the tin
(pan), then remove and cool
completely on a wire rack. Wrap
in plastic wrap or foil and store
in a cool place until required.

Rich Fruit Cake

This recipe makes a very moist rich cake suitable for any celebration. The cake can be made in stages, especially if time is short or if you are making more than one. It is easiest if the fruit is prepared and soaked overnight and the cake made the following day. Once the mixture is in the tin (pan), the surface may be covered with cling film (plastic wrap) and the cake stored in a cool place overnight if cooking is not possible on the day. The quantities have been carefully worked out so that the depth of each cake is the same. This is important when making several tiers for a wedding cake.

A classic rich fruit cake is traditionally used for christening cakes, as in the base for this delightful creation for a baby girl.

1 *Into a large mixing bowl place the raisins, sultanas (golden raisins), currants, glacé cherries, mixed (candied) peel, flaked almonds, lemon rind and juice, brandy or sherry. Mix all the ingredients together until well blended, then cover the bowl with cling film (plastic wrap). Leave for several hours or overnight if required.*

2 *Pre-heat the oven to 140°C/275°F/Gas 1 and prepare a deep cake tin (see Lining Cake Tins/Pans). Sift the flour and mixed spice into another mixing bowl. Add the ground almonds, sugar, butter, treacle (or molasses) and eggs. Mix together with a wooden spoon, then beat for 1–2 minutes until smooth and glossy. Alternatively, beat for 1 minute using an electric mixer.*

3 *Gradually add mixed fruit and fold into cake mixture using a plastic or wooden spatula until all the fruit has been evenly blended.*

4 *Spoon the mixture into the prepared tin (pan) and spread evenly. Give the container a few sharp bangs to level the mixture and to remove any air pockets. Smooth the surface with the back of a metal spoon, making a slight depression in the centre. The cake surface may be covered with cling film (plastic wrap) and left overnight in a cool place if required.*

5 *Bake the cake in the centre of the oven following the chart cooking time as a guide. Test the cake to see if it is cooked 30 minutes before the end of the cooking time. The cake should feel firm and, when a fine skewer is inserted into the centre, it should come out quite clean. If the cake is not cooked, retest it at 15-minute intervals. Remove the cake from the oven and allow it to cool in the tin (pan).*

6 *Turn the cake out of the tin (pan) but do not remove the lining paper as it helps to keep the moisture in. Spoon half quantity of brandy or sherry used in each cake over the top of the cooked cake and wrap in a double thickness of foil.*

STORING

Store the cake in a cool, dry place on its base with the top uppermost for a week. Unwrap the cake and spoon over the remaining brandy or sherry. Rewrap well and invert the cake. Store it upside down, so the brandy or sherry moistens the top and helps to keep it flat.

The cake will store well for up to 3 months. If it is going to be stored for this length of time, add the brandy or sherry a little at a time at monthly intervals.

RICH FRUIT CAKE CHART

Cake Tin Sizes	12 cm/5 in Square	15 cm/6 in Square	18 cm/7 in Square	20 cm/8 in Square	23 cm/9 in Square	25 cm/10 in Square	28 cm/11 in Square	30 cm/12 in Square
	15 cm/6 in Round	18 cm/7 in Round	20 cm/8 in Round	23 cm/9 in Round	25 cm/10 in Round	28 cm/11 in Round	30 cm/12 in Round	33 cm/13 in Round
INGREDIENTS								
Raisins	200 g/ 7 oz/ 1⅓ cups	250 g/ 9 oz/ 1¾ cups	325 g/ 11 oz/ 2 cups	375 g/ 13 oz/ 2½ cups	425 g/ 15 oz/ 2⅔ cups	575 g/ 1¼ lb/ 3¾ cups	675 g/ 1½ lb/ 4½ cups	800 g/ 1¾ lb/ 5¼ cups
Sultanas (golden raisins)	125 g/ 4 oz/ ¾ cup	175 g/ 6 oz/ 1¼ cups	225 g/ 8 oz/ 1½ cups	275 g/ 10 oz/ 1⅔ cups	350 g/ 12 oz/ 2¼ cups	475 g/ 1 lb 1 oz/ 3¼ cups	600 g/ 1 lb 5 oz/ 4 cups	675 g/ 1½ lb/ 4½ cups
Currants	75 g/ 3 oz/ ⅔ cup	125 g/ 4 oz/ ¾ cup	175 g/ 6 oz/ 1¼ cups	225 g/ 8 oz/ 1⅔ cups	275 g/ 10 oz/ 2 cups	400 g/ 14 oz/ 3 cups	475 g/ 1 lb 1 oz/ 3½ cups	575 g/ 1¼ lb/ 4 cups
Glacé cherries, halved	75 g/ 3 oz/ ½ cup	75 g/ 3 oz/ ½ cup	150 g/ 5 oz/ 1 cup	175 g/ 6 oz/ 1 cup	200 g/ 7 oz/ 1⅓ cups	225 g/ 8 oz/ 1½ cups	275 g/ 10 oz/ 1⅔ cups	350 g/ 12 oz/ 2¼ cups
Mixed peel	25 g/ 1 oz/ ¼ cup	40 g/ 1½ oz/ ⅓ cup	50 g/ 2 oz/ ⅓ cup	75 g/ 3 oz/ ½ cup	125 g/ 4 oz/ ¾ cup	175 g/ 6 oz/ 1 cup	225 g/ 8 oz/ 1½ cups	275 g/ 10 oz/ 1⅔ cups
Flaked almonds	25 g/ 1 oz/ ¼ cup	40 g/ 1½ oz/ ⅓ cup	50 g/ 2 oz/ ½ cup	75 g/ 3 oz/ ¾ cup	125 g/ 4 oz/ 1 cup	175 g/ 6 oz/ 1⅔ cup	225 g/ 8 oz/ 2¼ cups	275 g/ 10 oz/ 2¾ cups
Lemon rind, coarsely grated	5 ml/ 1 tsp/ 1 tsp	7.5 ml/ 1½ tsp/ 1½ tsp	10 ml/ 2 tsp/ 2 tsp	12 ml/ 2½ tsp/ 2½ tsp	15 ml/ ½ fl oz/ 1 tbsp	25 ml/ 1½ tbsp/ 1½ tbsp	25 ml/ 1½ tbsp/ 1½ tbsp	30 ml/ 2 tbsp/ 2 tbsp
Lemon juice	15 ml/ 1 tbsp/ 1 tbsp	25 ml/ 1½ tbsp/ 1½ tbsp	30 ml/ 2 tbsp/ 2 tbsp	40 ml/ 2½ tbsp/ 2½ tbsp	45 ml/ 3 tbsp/ 3 tbsp	60 ml/ 4 tbsp/ 4 tbsp	75 ml/ 5 tbsp/ 5 tbsp	90 ml/ 6 tbsp/ 6 tbsp
Brandy or sherry	15 ml/ 1 tbsp/ 1 tbsp	30 ml/ 2 tbsp/ 2 tbsp	45 ml/ 3 tbsp/ 3 tbsp	60 ml/ 4 tbsp/ 4 tbsp	75 ml/ 5 tbsp/ 5 tbsp	90 ml/ 6 tbsp/ 6 tbsp	105 ml/ 7 tbsp/ 7 tbsp	120 ml/ 8 tbsp/ ½ cup
Plain (all-purpose) flour	175 g/ 6 oz/ 1½ cups	200 g/ 7 oz/ 1¾ cups	250 g/ 9 oz/ 2¼ cups	325 g/ 11 oz/ 2¾ cups	400 g/ 14 oz/ 3½ cups	500 g/ 1 lb 2 oz/ 4½ cups	625 g/ 1 lb 6 oz/ 5½ cups	725 g/ 1 lb 10 oz/ 6½ cups
Ground mixed spice	5 ml/ 1 tsp/ 1 tsp	7.5 ml/ 1½ tsp/ 1½ tsp	12 ml/ 2½ tsp/ 2½ tsp	15 ml/ 1 tbsp/ 1 tbsp	18 ml/ 1¼ tbsp/ 1¼ tbsp	25 ml/ 1½ tbsp/ 1½ tbsp	30 ml/ 2 tbsp/ 2 tbsp	70 ml/ 3½ tbsp/ 3½ tbsp
Ground almonds	25 g/ 1 oz/ ¼ cup	40 g/ 1½ oz/ ⅓ cup	65 g/ 2½ oz/ ⅔ cup	125 g/ 4 oz/ 1¼ cups	150 g/ 5 oz/ 1⅓ cups	225 g/ 8 oz/ 2¼ cups	275 g/ 10 oz/ 2¾ cups	350 g/ 12 oz/ 3⅓ cups
Dark brown sugar	125 g/ 4 oz/ ¾ cup	150 g/ 5 oz/ 1 cup	200 g/ 7 oz/ 1⅓ cups	250 g/ 9 oz/ 1⅔ cups	350 g/ 12 oz/ 2¼ cups	475 g/ 1 lb 1 oz/ 3⅓ cups	575 g/ 1¼ lb/ 3¾ cups	650 g/ 1 lb 7 oz/ 4½ cups
Butter, softened	125 g/ 4 oz/ ½ cup	150 g/ 5 oz/ ⅔ cup	200 g/ 7 oz/ 1 cup	250 g/ 9 oz/ 1¼ cups	350 g/ 12 oz/ 1½ cups	475 g/ 1 lb 1 oz/ 2¼ cups	575 g/ 1¼ lb/ 2½ cups	650 g/ 1 lb 7 oz/ 3 cups
Black treacle (or molasses)	10 ml/ ½ tbsp/ ½ tbsp	15 ml/ 1 tbsp/ 1 tbsp	25 ml/ 1½ tbsp/ 1½ tbsp	30 ml/ 2 tbsp/ 2 tbsp	40 ml/ 2½ tbsp/ 2½ tbsp	45 ml/ 3 tbsp/ 3 tbsp	55 ml/ 3½ tbsp/ 3½ tbsp	60 ml/ 4 tbsp/ 4 tbsp
Eggs	2	3	4	5	6	7	8	10
Approx. Cooking Time	2¼–2½ hours	2½–2¾ hours	3–3½ hours	3¼–3¾ hours	3¾–4¼ hours	4–4½ hours	4½–5¼ hours	5¼–5¾ hours

Whisked Sponge Cake

This light sponge can be used for making Swiss rolls, cakes or gateaux.

Airy whisked sponge cake is the classic base for swiss rolls; here incorporating a cream and raspberry filling.

INGREDIENTS	2-EGG QUANTITY	3-EGG QUANTITY	4-EGG QUANTITY
● *Eggs*	2	3	4
● *Caster (superfine) sugar*	50 g/2 oz/¼ cup	75 g/3 oz/⅓ cup	125 g/4 oz/½ cup
● *Plain (all-purpose) flour*	50 g/2 oz/½ cup	75 g/3 oz/¾ cup	125 g/4 oz/1 cup

1 *Preheat the oven to 180°C/350°F/Gas 4. Prepare the tin (pan) according to the recipe.*

2 *Whisk together the eggs and sugar in a heatproof bowl until thoroughly blended. Place the bowl over a saucepan of simmering water and whisk until thick and pale. Remove the bowl from the saucepan and continue whisking until the mixture is cool and leaves a thick trail on the surface when the beaters are lifted.*

3 *Sift the flour onto the surface, add any desired flavourings and, using a plastic spatula, carefully fold the flour into the mixture until smooth.*

4 *Pour into a prepared tin (pan), tilt to level and bake as required.*

Butter Icing

This most popular and well-known icing is made quickly with butter and icing (confectioners') sugar. Add your choice of flavourings and colourings to vary the cake.

INGREDIENTS

Makes 450 g/1 lb/1 lb
- *125 g/4 oz/½ cup unsalted butter, softened*
- *225 g/8 oz/2 cups icing (confectioners') sugar, sifted*
- *10 ml/2 tsp/2 tsp milk*
- *5 ml/1 tsp/1 tsp vanilla essence (extract)*

Butter icing is a quick and attractive topping for a cake.

1 *Place the butter in a bowl. Using a wooden spoon or an electric mixer, beat until light and fluffy.*

2 *Stir in the icing (confectioners') sugar, milk and vanilla essence (extract), and/ or flavourings until evenly mixed, then beat well until light and smooth.*

3 *Spread the icing over the cake with a metal palette knife (spatula).*

CHOICE OF FLAVOURINGS

Citrus – replace milk and vanilla essence (extract) with orange, lemon or lime juice and 10 ml/2 tsp/2 tsp finely grated orange, lemon or lime rind. Omit the rind if the icing is to be piped.

Chocolate – 15 ml/1 tbsp/1 tbsp cocoa powder blended with 15 ml/ 1 tbsp/1 tbsp boiling water, cooled
Coffee – 10 ml/2 tsp/2 tsp coffee granules blended with 15 ml/1 tbsp/ 1 tbsp boiling water, cooled

Chocolate Fudge Icing

A rich glossy icing which sets like chocolate fudge, it is versatile enough to smoothly coat, swirl or pipe, depending on the temperature of the icing when it is used.

INGREDIENTS

Makes 450 g/1 lb/1 lb
- 125 g/4 oz/4 squares plain (semisweet) chocolate
- 50 g/2 oz/¼ cup unsalted butter
- 1 egg, beaten
- 175 g/6 oz/1 cup icing (confectioners') sugar, sifted

Chocolate fudge icing is smooth and sumptuous, with a rich dark colour that contrasts beautifully with fresh flowers in a simple but effective decoration.

1 Place the chocolate and butter in a heatproof bowl over a saucepan of hot water.

2 Stir occasionally with a wooden spoon until melted. Add the egg and beat until the mixture is smooth.

3 Remove the bowl from the saucepan and stir in the icing (confectioners') sugar, then beat until smooth and glossy.

4 Pour immediately over the cake for a smooth finish, or leave to cool for a thicker spreading or piping consistency as shown here.

American Frosting

A light marshmallow icing which crisps on the outside when left to dry, this versatile frosting may be swirled or peaked into a soft coating.

Makes 350 g/12 oz/¾ lb
- 1 egg white
- 30 ml/2 tbsp/2 tbsp water
- 15 ml/1 tbsp/1 tbsp golden syrup (light corn syrup)
- 5 ml/1 tsp/1 tsp cream of tartar
- 175 g/6 oz/1 cup icing (confectioners') sugar, sifted

American frosting makes a light, fluffy yet crisp topping, its soft white contrasting well with chocolate caraque.

1 Place the egg white, water, golden syrup (light corn syrup) and cream of tartar in a heatproof bowl. Whisk together until thoroughly blended.

2 Stir the icing (confectioners') sugar into the mixture and place the bowl over a saucepan of simmering water. Whisk until the mixture becomes thick and white.

3 Remove the bowl from the saucepan and continue to whisk the frosting until cool and thick, and the mixture stands up in soft peaks.

4 Use immediately to fill or cover cakes.

Homemade Marzipan

INGREDIENTS

Makes 450 g/1 lb/1 lb

- *225 g/8 oz/2¼ cups ground almonds*
- *125 g/4 oz/½ cup caster (superfine) sugar*
- *125 g/4 oz/¾ cup icing (confectioners') sugar, sieved (sifted)*
- *5 ml/1 tsp/1 tsp lemon juice*
- *few drops almond flavouring*
- *1 (size 4) egg, or 1 (size 2) egg white*

Marzipan is extremely versatile; here it has been used in place of icing for this unusual Christmas cake.

1 *Place the ground almonds, caster (superfine) and icing (confectioners') sugars into a bowl. Stir until evenly mixed.*

2 *Make a 'well' in the centre and add the lemon juice, almond flavouring and enough egg or egg white to mix to a soft but firm dough, using a wooden spoon.*

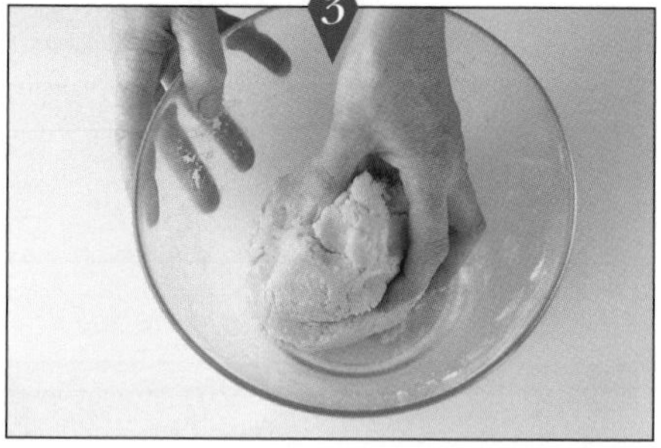

3 *Form the marzipan into a ball. Lightly dust a surface with icing (confectioners') sugar and knead the marzipan until smooth and free from cracks.*

4 *Wrap the marzipan in cling film (plastic wrap) or store in a plastic bag until ready for use. Tint with food colouring if required, and use for moulding shapes or covering cakes.*

MARZIPAN CHART

Cake Tin Sizes	12 cm/5 in Square	15 cm/6 in Square	18 cm/7 in Square	20 cm/8 in Square	23 cm/9 in Square	25 cm/10 in Square	28 cm/11 in Square	30 cm/12 in Square
	15 cm/6 in Round	18 cm/7 in Round	20 cm/8 in Round	23 cm/9 in Round	25 cm/10 in Round	28 cm/11 in Round	30 cm/12 in Round	33 cm/13 in Round
QUANTITIES								
Apricot glaze	25 ml/ 1½ tbsp/ 1½ tbsp	30 ml/ 2 tbsp/ 2 tbsp	40 ml/ 2½ tbsp/ 2½ tbsp	45 ml/ 3 tbsp/ 3 tbsp	55 ml/ 3½ tbsp/ 3½ tbsp	60 ml/ 4 tbsp/ 4 tbsp	75 ml/ 4½ tbsp/ 4½ tbsp	75 ml/ 5 tbsp/ 5 tbsp
Marzipan	450 g/ 1 lb/ 1 lb	675 g/ 1½ lb/ 1½ lb	800g/ 1¾ lb/ 1¾ lb	900 g/ 2 lb/ 2 lb	1.1 kg/ 2½ lb/ 2½ lb	1.5 kg/ 3¼ lb/ 3¼ lb	1.8 kg/ 4 lb/ 4 lb	1.9 kg/ 4¼ lb/ 4¼ lb

Royal Icing 1

This icing made with fresh egg whites is traditionally used to cover celebration cakes. Depending upon its consistency, it may be used for flat icing, peaked icing or piping designs on to cakes.

Makes 450 g/1 lb/1½ cups
- *2 egg whites*
- *1.5 ml/¼ tsp/¼ tsp lemon juice*
- *450 g/1 lb/3 cups icing (confectioners') sugar, sieved (sifted)*
- *5 ml/1 tsp/1 tsp glycerine*

Royal Icing Consistencies

The consistency of royal icing varies for different uses. Stiff icing is necessary for piping, slightly softer for flat icing or peaked icing, and slacker for run-outs.

PIPING CONSISTENCY
When a wooden spoon is drawn out of the icing, it should form a fine, sharp point, termed as 'sharp peak'. This consistency flows easily for piping but retains a definite shape produced by the nozzle.

FLAT OR PEAKED ICING CONSISTENCY
When the spoon is drawn out of the icing it should form a fine point which curves over at the end, termed as 'soft peak'. This consistency spreads smoothly and creates a flat finish, but also pulls up into sharp or soft peaks.

RUN-OUTS
Use soft peak consistency to pipe the outlines, and thick cream consistency to fill in the shapes. This consistency flows to fill in the run-outs, but holds a rounded shape within the piped lines.

Peaked royal icing has been used to coat little fruit cakes for a witty and attractive festive gift.

1 *Place the egg whites and lemon juice in a clean bowl. Using a clean wooden spoon, stir to break up the egg whites. Add sufficient icing (confectioners') sugar and mix well to form the consistency of unwhipped cream.*

2 *Continue mixing and adding small quantities of sugar every few minutes, until the desired consistency has been reached. Mix well after each addition of sugar.*

3 *Stir in the glycerine until the icing is well blended.*

How to Marzipan a Cake for Sugarpaste (Fondant Icing)

APRICOT GLAZE

It is always a good idea to make a large quantity of apricot glaze, especially when making celebration cakes. Use for brushing the cakes before applying the marzipan, or for glazing fruits on gateaux and cakes.

INGREDIENTS

Makes 450 g/1 lb/1 lb
- *450 g/1 lb/1½ cups apricot jam*
- *45 ml/3 tbsp/3 tbsp water*

1 *Place jam and water into a saucepan, heat gently, stirring occasionally until melted. Boil rapidly for 1 minute, then strain through a sieve (strainer).*

2 *Rub through as much fruit as possible, using a wooden spoon. Discard the skins left in the sieve (strainer).*

STORING

Pour the glaze into a clean, hot jar, seal with a clean lid and cool. Refrigerate for up to 2 months.

1 *Unwrap the cake and remove the lining paper. Place the cake on a cakeboard and roll the top with a rolling pin to flatten slightly.*

2 *Brush the top and sides of the cake with apricot glaze (see above), and dust the surface lightly with sieved (sifted) icing (confectioners') sugar.*

3 *Knead the marzipan into a smooth ball. Roll out to a 5 mm/¼ in thickness, to match the shape of the cake, and large enough to cover the top and sides, about 5–7.5 cm/2–3 in larger. Make sure the marzipan moves freely, then roll the marzipan loosely around the rolling pin.*

4 Place the supported marzipan over the cake and carefully unroll so that the marzipan falls evenly over the cake. Working from the centre of the cake, carefully smooth the marzipan over the top and down the sides, lifting the edges slightly to allow the marzipan to fit at the base of the cake without stretching or tearing the top edge.

5 Using a sharp knife, trim the excess marzipan from the base of the cake, cutting down on to the board.

6 Using clean, dry hands, gently rub the top of the cake in circular movements to make a smooth glossy finish to the marzipan.

7 Leave in a warm, dry place for at least 2 hours before covering with sugarpaste (fondant).

To Cover Any Shaped Cake with Sugarpaste (Fondant)

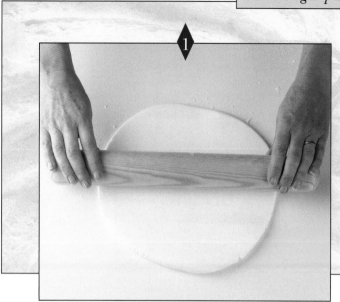

1 *Place the marzipanned cake, on the cakeboard, onto a turntable and brush the surface evenly with a little sherry or cooled boiled water. Dust a work surface with sieved (sifted) icing (confectioners') sugar to prevent the sugarpaste from sticking. Roll out the sugarpaste (fondant) to 5 mm/¼ in thickness, using more sieved (sifted) icing (confectioners') sugar if necessary, to the chosen shape of the cake.*

2 *Trim the sugarpaste (fondant) to 6.5 cm/2½ in larger than the top of the cake, making sure the icing moves freely. Lift the sugarpaste carefully over the top of the cake, supported by a rolling pin. Brush off any excess icing (confectioners') sugar. Unroll the sugarpaste over the cake to cover evenly.*

3 *Dust your hands with cornflour (cornstarch), and smooth the icing over the top and then down the sides of the cake. Ease the excess icing toward the base, excluding any air bubbles between the surfaces. Trim off excess icing at base of cake using a small knife.*

4 *Dust your hands with more cornflour (cornstarch), and gently rub the surface of the sugarpaste in circular movements to make it smooth and glossy. Place the cake in a cake box and leave in a warm, dry place to dry the sugarpaste.*

5 *Knead the trimmings together and seal in cling film (plastic wrap) or a plastic bag and use to cover the cakeboard, or for decorations.*

To Cover Any Shaped Cakeboard with Sugarpaste (Fondant)

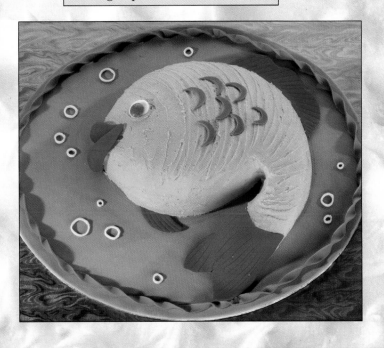

Complete the effect of a novelty or classic cake by continuing the coloured fondant or sugarpaste covering onto the cakeboard.

1 Lightly dust a surface with icing (confectioners') sugar. Tint the sugarpaste (fondant) to the required colour to match the cake. Brush the cakeboard with a little apricot glaze.

2 Roll out the sugarpaste (fondant) to 5 mm/¼ in thickness to the shape of the cakeboard. Ensure the sugarpaste moves freely and lift over the cakeboard. Dust your hands with cornflour (cornstarch), and smooth the surface, trimming off excess icing using a small palette knife (spatula). Keep the blade level with the edge of the board and take care to keep the edge of the sugarpaste (fondant) straight.

3 Leave the iced board in a warm place overnight to dry. Then place the iced cake carefully in position.

FOOD COLOURINGS AND TINTS

Food colourings and tints have changed dramatically over the last few years. At one time food colourings were only available in bottles in a range of primary colours. These liquid colours are still available from most supermarkets and shops and are adequate for tinting icings, frosting, butter icing, marzipan and sugarpaste. With careful blending many other colours and shades can be achieved. Since the colourings are fairly diluted, it is impossible to achieve a richer colour without diluting the consistency of the icing. So for stronger colours, concentrated food colouring pastes produce better results.

PASTE, POWDER AND LIQUID COLOURS

In specialist cake-icing and decorating shops, food colourings are available in a far greater range. Good quality colours appear as pastes, powders and liquids. They are very concentrated and need to be added drop by drop, using a cocktail stick to stir and carefully tint the icing to a delicate shade. An exceptional variety of colours are available so there is no need to blend the colours to obtain the shade of icing you want. Since they are so concentrated, the consistency of the icing is not affected. The colours are also permanent and do not fade.

Remember that food colourings, when added to icings or kneaded into marzi-pan or sugarpaste, change on standing and dry a deeper or a lighter colour than when first mixed. Colour sample amounts of icing in the daylight and leave them for at least 15 minutes to assess if you have achieved the desired colour. If you are matching icing with fabrics or flowers, allow coloured samples to dry thoroughly before deciding. If several batches of coloured icing are to be made, keep some icing in reserve so the colour can be matched. Always remember that a cake should look edible, so keep the colours to pastel shades – a hint of colour is better than too much.

Celebration cakes may require more subtle shading and tinting. Moulded and cut-out flowers, sugar pieces and cakes' surfaces can now be coloured with 'blossom tints', or painted with 'lustre colours'

when the flowers, sugar pieces or icings are dry. This also gives you an opportunity to add colour at the last minute, and prevents the risk of colours running into the icing when the atmosphere is damp. These products also hold their colour without fading. Such specialist food colours are available only from cake-decorating shops.

FOOD-COLOURING PENS

These pens look like fibre-tip pens but are filled with edible food colourings. They come in a range of primary colours as well as black, brown and purple. Their uses are endless, especially for quickly decorating, writing or applying details to models or sugar pieces.

Use them like a pen to write or draw a design onto dry royal icing run-outs, small sugar plaques or even to mark a design directly onto an iced cake. But these pens are indelible – so make no mistakes!

Marzipan or sugarpaste (fondant) is easily tinted with food colouring; break off small pieces and work in gradually until evenly blended.

Marbling

Sugarpaste (fondant) lends itself to tinting in all shades, and a very effective way of colouring is to marble the paste. Use it to cover a cake and the cakeboard completely and use the trimmings for cut-out or moulded decorations.

1 *Add a few drops of food colouring in drops over the icing.*

2 *Do not knead the food colouring fully into the icing.*

3 *When it is rolled out, the colour is dispersed in such a way that it gives a marbled appearance to the sugarpaste (fondant).*

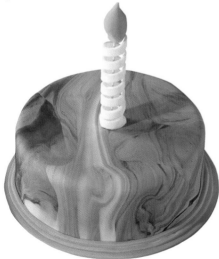

Marbling is a wonderful effect easily achieved with sugarpaste or fondant and edible food colourings, as shown with this blue and orange candle-shaped novelty cake.

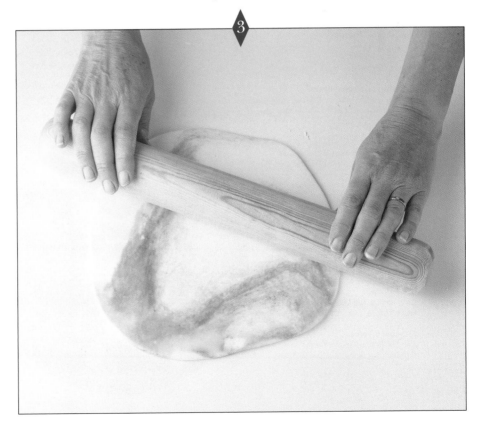

Great Britain

THE BRITISH SUGARCRAFT GUILD
Wellington House, Messeter Place, Eltham, London SE9 5DP.

CAKE ART LTD
Wholesale suppliers of icings and equipment. Unit 16, Crown Close, Crown Industrial Estate, Priors Wood, Taunton, Somerset TA2 8RX.

SUGARCRAFT SUPPLIERS PME (HARROW) LTD
Suppliers of decorating equipment. Brember Road, South Harrow, Middlesex HA2 8UN.

JF RENSHAW LTD
Suppliers of icings. Locks Lane, Mitcham, Surrey CR4 2XG.

ESSEX ICING CENTRE
Suppliers of materials and equipment. 20 Western Road, Billericay, Essex CM12 9DZ.

INVICTA BAKEWARE LTD
Manufacturers and suppliers of bakery equipment. Westgate Business Park, Westgate Carr Road, Pickering, North Yorkshire Y018 8LX.

CRANHAM CATERING
Suppliers of materials and equipment. 95 Front Lane, Cranham, Upminster, Essex RM14 1XN.

CRAIG MILLAR
Suppliers of icings. Stadium Road, Bromborough, Wirral, Merseyside LO2 3NU.

PROMODEM LTD
Technical consultancy and suppliers of cake tilters. 141 Grange Road, Great Burstead, Billericay, Essex CM11 2SA.

SQUIRES KITCHEN
Squire House, 3 Waverley Lane, Farnham, Surrey GU9 8BB.

E RUSSUM & SONS
Edward House, Tenter Street, Rotherham.

THE HOUSE OF SUGARCRAFT
Suppliers of flower cutters, powder and paste colours and piping tubes. Unit 10, Broxhead Industrial Estate, Lindford Road, Bordon, Hampshire GU35 ONY.

CEL CAKES
Suppliers of modelling tools, containers and display cabinets. Springfield House, Gate Helmsley, York, North Yorkshire YO4 1NF.

JENNY CAMPBELL TRADING/B R MATTHEWS AND SON
12 Gypsy Hill, Upper Norwood, London SE19 1NN.

CYNTHIA VENN
3 Anker Lane, Stubbington, Fareham, Hampshire PO14 3HF.

KNIGHTSBRIDGE BUSINESS CENTRE (WILTON UK)
Knightsbridge, Cheltenham, Gloucestershire GL51 9TA.

RAINBOW RIBBONS
Unit D5, Romford Seedbed Centre, Davidson Way, Romford, Essex RM7 OAZ.

North America

ICES (INTERNATIONAL CAKE EXPLORATION SOCIETY)
Membership enquiries: 3087–30th St. S.W., Ste.101, Grandville, MI 49418.

MAID OF SCANDINAVIA
Equipment, supplies, courses, magazine Mailbox News. 3244 Raleigh Avenue, Minneapolis, MN 55416.

WILTON ENTERPRISES INC
2240 West 75th Street, Woodridge, Illinois 60517.

HOME CAKE ARTISTRY INC
1002 North Central, Suite 511, Richardson, Texas 75080.

LORRAINE'S INC
148 Broadway, Hanover, MA 02339.

CREATIVE TOOLS LTD
3 Tannery Court, Richmond Hill, Ontario, Canada L4C 7V5.

MCCALL'S SCHOOL OF CAKE DECORATING INC
3810 Bloor Street, Islington, Ontario, Canada M9B 6C2..

Australia

AUSTRALIAN NATIONAL CAKE DECORATORS' ASSOCIATION
PO Box 321, Plympton, SA 5038.

CAKE DECORATING ASSOCIATION OF VICTORIA
President, Shirley Vaas, 4 Northcote Road, Ocean Grove, Victoria 3226.

CAKE DECORATING GUILD OF NEW SOUTH WALES
President, Fay Gardiner, 4 Horsley Cres, Melba, Act, 2615.

CAKE DECORATING ASSOCIATION OF TASMANIA
Secretary, Jenny Davis, 29 Honolulu Street, Midway Point, Tasmania 7171.

CAKE DECORATOR'S ASSOCIATION OF SOUTH AUSTRALIA
Secretary, Lorraine Joliffe, Pindari, 12 Sussex Crescent, Morphet Vale, SA 5162.

CAKE ORNAMENT CO
156 Alfred Street, Fortitude Valley, Brisbane 4006.

INDEX

ACKNOWLEDGEMENTS

Janice Murfitt would like to thank the following: Mavis Giles for her unfailing ability to type illegible copy at a minute's notice; Jean Ainger for supplying equipment and sugarcraft props for photography; Cake Fayre, 11 Saddlers Walk, 44 East Street, Chichester, W Sussex, PO19 1HQ (Tel. 01243 771857).

Louise Pickford and Sarah Maxwell would like to thank Teresa Goldfinch for her assistance with home economy.